SOUL
OF THE
CITY

THE PIKE PLACE PUBLIC MARKET

SOUL OF THE CITY

THE PIKE PLACE PUBLIC MARKET

Alice Shorett and Murray Morgan

THE MARKET FOUNDATION
in association with the
UNIVERSITY OF WASHINGTON PRESS
SEATTLE AND LONDON

THE MARKET FOUNDATION

85 Pike Street, Room 500

Seattle, WA 98101

www.pikeplacemarket.org

UNIVERSITY OF WASHINGTON PRESS

PO Box 50096

Seattle, WA 98145

www.washington.edu/uwpress

Library of Congress Cataloging-in-Publication Data

Shorett, Alice.

Soul of the city : the Pike Place Public Market / Alice Shorett and Murray Morgan.

p. cm.

*"This is an updated edition of The Pike Place Market : people, politics, and produce
originally published by Pacific Search Press in 1982"—T.p. verso.*

  Includes bibliographical references.

  ISBN-13: 978-0-295-98746-0 (pbk. : alk. paper)

  ISBN-10: 0-295-98746-4 (pbk. : alk. paper)

*1. Pike Place Market (Seattle, Wash.)—History. 2. Markets—Washington (State)—
Seattle—History. I. Morgan, Murray Cromwell, 1916– II. Shorett, Alice. Pike Place
Market. III. Title. IV. Title: Pike Place Public Market.*

HF5472.U7S47   2007

381'.1809797772—dc22   2007018073

*The paper used in this publication meets the minimum requirements of American National
Standard for Information Sciences—Permanence of Paper for Printed Library Materials,
ANSI Z39.48-1984.*

*Photo credits appear with individual photos except the following: Frank Natsuhara, page
10; Mary Randlett, page 8; and Jack Morley, pages 174–75.*

*On the title page, a 1920 postcard shows the Pike Place Public Market in the early days
of the all-automobile era. The street was cobbled, the pedestrians were all hatted, but the
Market is instantly recognizable. (City of Seattle)*

Contents

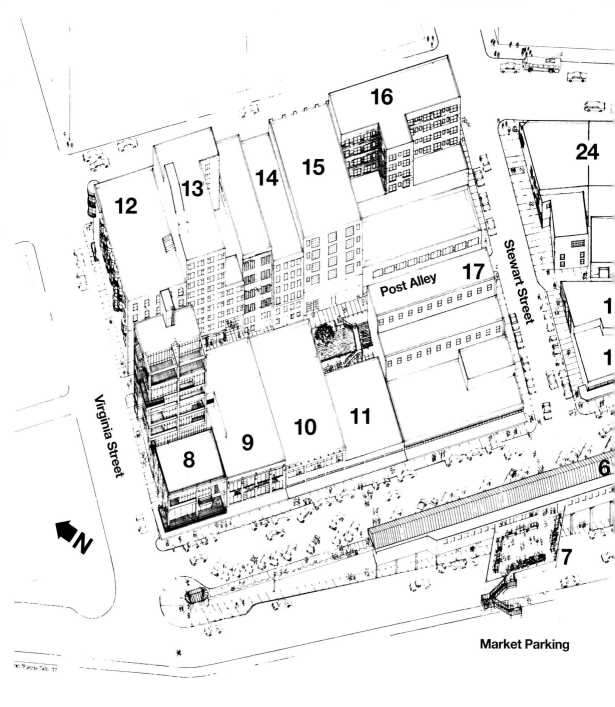

1. Economy Market
2. LaSalle Hotel/Apartments
3. Hillclimb Corridor
4. Leland Hotel/Apartments
5. Main Market/Fairley
6. North Arcade
7. Desimone Bridge
8. Pike and Virginia Building
9. Champion Building
10. Soames Paper/combined in renovation to Soames/Dunn Buildings
11. Dunn Seed/combined in renovation to Soames/Dunn Buildings
12. Livingston Apartments
13. Baker Building

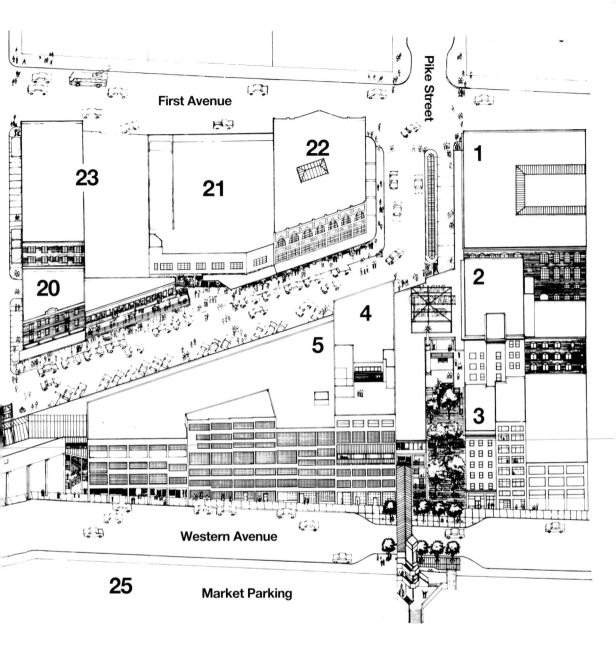

First Avenue

Pike Street

23

22

21

1

2

20

4

5

3

Western Avenue

25   Market Parking

Acknowledgments

We wish to thank the following people for their aid in making this book possible:

Richard Desimone, Mondo Desimone, Mrs. George Maselli, Torger Birkland, Lois Austin, Harry Foster, Mary Bonamy, Caroline Goodwin, John Clise, Joan Paulson, Robert Gill, Mrs. Lloyd Graves, Joe Ford, Robert Hitchman, Tony Genzale, Thomas Upper, Carly Westcott, Willard Soames, David Mossafer, Tom Iwasaki, Fred Rogers, Morris Hannan, Dr. Sussman, Tim Manring, Frank Miller, Gerry Johnson, Randy Revelle, Victor Steinbrueck, Harriet Sherburne, Ken MacInnes, John Turnbull, Virginia Felton, Laurie Olin, James Mason, Dorothy Revelle, Richard Brustiwicz, Lou Anne Kirby, Susan Mersereau, Edward Delanty, Margaret Wherrette, Peter Steinbrueck, Marlys Erickson, Carol Binder, Michael Yaeger, Jackson Schmidt, Len Barson, Shelly Yapp, Fred Tausend, Barbara Bonamy, Jerry Thonn, Paul Dunn, David Harrison, Charles Dunsire, Vicki Gates, Paul Dorpat, and Nancy Pryor.

We'd also like to thank Evelyn Edens of the *Seattle Times*; staff at the University of Washington Special Collections; librarians at the Seattle Municipal Archives, Office of the City Clerk; librarians at the King County Clerk's Office; photographers, and those who opened their books, Rosa Morgan, David Shorett, Peter Shorett, and Mark Shorett.

Mary Randlett deserves special recognition for her photographs of the Market and her help in assembling all of the photographs for this book.

Foreword

For all of us who love Seattle's historic Pike Place Market, its 100th birthday is a time for celebration, as well as expectation of the next one hundred Market years. Just how has the nation's oldest continuously operated farmers' market survived for so long and retained its authenticity and distinction as one of the great public markets of the world? What changes will the Market have to endure to survive for another one hundred years?

The 1907 ordinance that created the public market at Pike Place, sponsored by Councilman Thomas P. Revelle, reflected the city's determination to cut out the middleman and bring fresh produce grown by local farmers directly to consumers.

In the 1960s, the Market, aging and run-down, was saved from the wrecking ball of "urban removal" by a tenacious group of citizens led by my father Victor Steinbrueck, culminating in a successful citizens' initiative in May 1971. An historic district was created to protect the farmer's market and its traditional uses, and an infusion of federal dollars, thanks to U.S. Senator Warren G. Magnuson, was used to restore the core Market buildings.

So, who then, would have imagined that history would repeat itself in the 1980s when a group of New York tax-credit investors calling themselves the Urban Group would take claim to ownership of the Market, and threaten dramatic rent increases that would drive out farmers and traditional small, owner-operated businesses?

Soul of the City: The Pike Place Public Market, by Alice Shorett and Murray Morgan, tells the story of the Market's colorful, illustrious past; the episodic challenges to its survival; and the story of those who fought to protect the Market from nefarious forces and changing times that could easily have destroyed it.

The Pike Place Market of my youth, when my father was fighting the decade-long battle to save it, was a different place in a different time. But I can almost still taste the fresh sweet carrots grown locally by Mama Verde, the sticks of imported pepperoni from DeLaurenti's Italian Market, the Scandia's homemade Swedish pancakes with lingonberries and whipped cream, and the bowls of spicy hot Sopa de Camarones served up by old Senor Ramón Palaez from a steaming kettle behind the bar stool counter of the Copacabana Café—mmm, good!

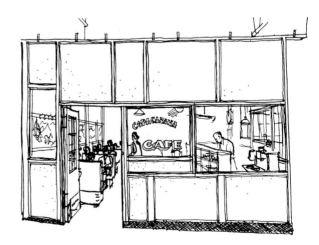

Yes, the sights, sounds, tastes, and smells endure, just as the Market does today.

Peter Steinbrueck
April 2007

ABOVE: *Sketch of the Copacabana Cafe by Victor Steinbrueck, from* Market Sketchbook.

Chapter 1 | SEED TIME

August is Seattle's dry month, more or less, but it rained on the evening of August 16, 1907, and the dawn of the 17th proved dismal. The clouds were heavy as clay; such streets as were cobbled or planked shone damply, and those unpaved squished with mud. Gulls wheeled overhead, their mewing mournful.

Under a sky that threatened more rain, H. O. Blanchard, who had a farm near Renton, drove his mud-splattered wagon into town, north along Western Avenue, a plank road still partly on pilings, past the warehouse of the commission men who bought produce from the farmers for wholesale to grocers, restaurants, and hotels. Steam rose from the horse's back as it plodded up the incline to Pike Place, which the Seattle city council had just designated as a public market.

Blanchard did not know what to expect. This was the first day of the experiment with the producer-to-consumer market. He had received a flyer outlining the rules established by the Seattle Department of Streets, which was officially responsible for the operation of the new facility: wagons arriving first had the choice of positions; wagons were to be placed five feet apart and backed against the curbs; the farmer must provide a box for refuse, and there was to be no shouting of wares. A policeman would be present to maintain order.

This simple list of market rules did not prepare Blanchard or the blue-coated policeman for what happened. A waiting crowd of fifty or so shoppers, most of them women, some fashionably dressed, all carrying market baskets, pushed the cop aside, stampeded to the wagon, and bought out the whole load before the wagon could be maneuvered to the curb.

Not long afterwards Antonio Ditore had a similar experience. He had come to Seattle from southern Italy and still had an old country touch to his English when he recalled opening day some years later:

I started work on my land and buy wagon and a horse and I go around First Avenue, Second Avenue, around the houses sell lettuce, radishes, green onions, all that stuff. Policeman come. He say, "You got no right, you got no license."
I said, "I got a few vegetables and I want to get some money to buy some flour to make bread. We have to live somehow." I don't know. I just started.
"Oh," the policeman said, "You cannot do that, you cannot do that." But then you know what he tell me? "Tomorrow open the Pike Place Market. You go over there."

Thats what he tell me, this policeman. And I did. I put the cart up by that building, the Leland Hotel, that was there when we get there. The back of there the people come a runnin' and I give some things without a paper bag. And they was glad to get it. And now I think in an hour there I make seven, eight dollars.

Throughout the morning, shoppers and curiosity seekers arrived by the hundreds. Most came by streetcar, disembarking at First and Pike, but others arrived in carriages, on bicycles, and two or three chugged up in automobiles. They milled on the board sidewalks, leaned against the forest of poles supporting electric lines, telephone lines, trolley lines. They admired the view of the waterfront with its slanted finger piers, tall ships, and small steamers. They studied posters on the board fences ("Headlion Overalls—Worn by the World's Most Famous Railroad"). But they found little to buy. After Blanchard and Ditore, only a half-dozen or so farmers

FACING PAGE: *Wholesalers on Western Avenue controlled food prices in Seattle before the city set aside Pike Place as a public market. (Photo by Asahel Curtis, University of Washington Libraries, Special Collections, A Curtis 14613)*

ABOVE: *Tony Ditore was 100 years old when photographed in 1978, but he vividly recalled carting produce to the Public Market opening day in 1907. (Photo by Nick Jahn)*

came to the market. Those who did were overwhelmed by their reception.

The next time I come to this place," one told a reporter, "I'm going to get police protection or put my wagon on stilts. I got rid of everything all right, but I didn't really sell a turnip. You see, those society women stormed my wagon, crawled over the wheels and crowded me off to a respectable distance, say 20 feet. When I got back the wagon was swept as clean as a good housewife's parlor, and there in a bushel basket was a quart of silver. Even if I didn't have the opportunity to so much as put a price on an ear of corn, it gave me a good price for my vegetables."

Others were not so lucky. One of the peddlers—men who drove carts with produce purchased from the wholesalers—resented competition from the producers, climbed onto a wagon, and began passing out the farmer's vegetables and fruit to the crowd. He was pulled off the wagon by some of the spectators. Another farmer complained that his produce was spilled onto the street and stomped by some men and boys he suspected of trying to touch off a riot.

But, one way or another, all of the produce found takers. By 11 A.M. there were thousands of shoppers with nothing to buy and no more carts. The first day of the Pike Place Public Market had been a clamorous fiasco—but promising.

Some three thousand farms were scattered throughout King County, and as many more were on islands linked to Seattle by small steamers of the mosquito fleet. About half the farmers were native-born Americans; the rest were new arrivals, mostly from Europe, though there were some Chinese and a growing number of Japanese and Filipinos.

The Americans and the Germans were sprinkled over all parts of the county; other immigrants tended to pool in ethnic groups—Italians clustered in Rainier Valley, Asians along the White River, Scandinavians and South Slavs often close to salt water.

No soil seemed too unpromising to attract a tiller. The prairies of glacial drift with their grass cover and scattered trees remained deceptively inviting, though experience had demonstrated such land was more suited for grazing than farming. A generation of stump ranchers had proved that logged-off land was better for conifers than cauliflower, but land-hungry newcomers still struggled to burn out the roots of fir and cedar to make

room for root crops. The best farmland lay in the valleys, where the mountain streams slowed and meandered as they approached the south and, during flood, deposited volcanic ash and decayed vegetation on the fields. So, though farms lay in an arc around the city, most of Seattle's farm produce came from the valleys of the White and the Duwamish, and of the Cedar and the little Black, which drained Lake Washington before the lake was lowered in 1916.

The farms were small, the work endless, the hours "from can't see to can't see," but the bottomlands were rich, and a man with a strong back and a footburner, as they called their one-share plows, could produce a surplus. They built big barns and small houses. Once or twice a week during the growing season, the farmers would roll out of bed about 4 A.M., feed their teams as the roosters began to crow, hitch their horses to wagons and carts loaded the night before, and start for town.

On clear days, the rivers beside the dirt roads steamed with morning mist, the mountain glowed pastel then whitened as the sun rose higher, and the air grew heavy with the scents of growth. Even in summer, mud was more often a problem than dust, and when it was raining, the trip was long. The valley roads converged into Marginal

---

ABOVE: *Farmers called their one-share plows "footburners." Handling one called for a strong back and willing horses. (State Library Collection, Washington State Archives)*

FACING PAGE: *The rich soil of the Black, the White, and the Duwamish valleys yielded enormous vegetables. (Washington State Historical Society, photo by Asahel Curtis, 37262)*

ABOVE: *Seattle was booming in the early years of the twentieth century. Some farmers were able to add to their spreads, build houses and outbuildings, and even have their prosperity recorded on stereopticon slides. (Sue Olsen Collection and Marie Swenson Collection)*

FACING PAGE: *Stacks of crates outside the commission houses on Western Avenue symbolize the importance of the wholesale dealers in King County's market economy. (Photo by Asahel Curtis, University of Washington Libraries, Special Collections, A Curtis 00973)*

Way, west of Beacon Hill and east of the Duwamish. The line of carts moved to The Lots, a three-square block area around Sixth Avenue and King Street. There, farmers who intended to peddle their wares door-to-door swapped produce with men who had raised different crops, and everybody exchanged hints about husbandry and complaints about prices.

From The Lots, some made deliveries to hotels and restaurants, others headed into the residential districts to hawk their vegetables and fruit, but the majority went to Western Avenue, better known as Produce Row, where the wholesale houses were located. Few farmers could afford to spend a day or two a week making sales. Instead, they sold through the commission houses, leaving produce with a wholesaler and receiving a percentage of the price brought when it was sold. If the price was high, the farmer received what had been projected when he talked to the wholesaler; if the price was low, so was his share; if no buyer was found, the farmer got nothing and his produce wilted, rotted, and became worthless.

At best the system was frustrating. At worst it was shot through with fraud and corruption. Since there certainly was some cheating, rumors of cheating tended to be believed. Commission firms were alleged to dump into the bay produce consigned by farmers who demanded high percentages, thus raising the price they received for produce sold to the commission houses by more timorous farmers who accepted lower percentages as their share. Some

wholesalers were accused of selling all a farmer's produce, then showing him a pile of spoiled vegetables that they claimed were part of his delivery. Many wholesalers were slow to pay even the pittance the grower was supposed to receive.

While farmers accused the middlemen of paying them too little, consumers complained that food prices were too high—and rising. The climax came when prices went up sharply between the summers of 1906 and 1907. Cherries cost six cents a pound in July 1906, ten cents in 1907; onions went from ten cents a pound to a dollar.

This rise in food costs coincided with the boom in Puget Sound lumber prices following the San Francisco earthquake and fire in April 1906, but this was also the era of President Theodore Roosevelt's trust-busting campaigns. Consumers suspected that food prices were controlled by a combine of commission houses. The seeds of such doubts were fertilized by the farmers' complaints that the growers were receiving less for their produce than they had a year earlier. Not surprisingly, the situation attracted the attention of a reform-minded politician and a crusading newspaper editor.

The reformer was Thomas P. Revelle, a round-faced, brown-haired, bushy-eyebrowed man of thirty-eight. Born in Maryland of French Huguenot stock (one of his ancestors led a pilgrimage to the Holy Land in the twelfth century, another was driven from France for opposing the established church, another came to Maryland with Lord Baltimore, and yet another helped organize the Republican party), Revelle proved to be a late bloomer in education, law, and politics. He was twenty-five before graduating from Western Maryland College in 1893, and thirty-five when he received a law degree from the University of Washington. He then spent three years as a Methodist minister. Not until 1906 did he begin to practice law. In June of that same year he was elected to the city council.

A Republican and disciple of Teddy Roosevelt (in 1912 he was one of the four original signers of the petition for organization of the Progressive party in Washington), Revelle took an immediate interest in the farm price controversy. Scholarly by nature, earnest, a do-gooder if ever there was one (his law school thesis was on "The Moral Obligation of a Contract"), he reviewed the history of farmers' markets from ancient Rome to contemporary Covent Garden. The best way to hold down prices and get fresh produce to the consumer, he decided, was to eliminate the middleman by making it easy for the farmer to sell directly to the public.

"When I saw this condition," he said later, "I felt that I must do something to obtain a public market . . . I knew not how the matter could be accomplished, but I was determined, if it took the whole of my public life, to have a market."

Revelle next learned that in 1896, before he arrived in Seattle, the city council had passed an ordinance authorizing the designation of some area as a public market. The ordinance, a product of the depression of 1893–97, had never been implemented, partly because of a controversy over provisions establishing a high license fee for peddlers and prohibiting any door-to-door sales during hours the public market was open. During the boom period of the Klondike gold rush the market idea lay dormant. Now Revelle reawakened it.

The tideflats were being firmed up with fill from the first stage of the downtown regrade project. The street department had just completed Western Avenue as a planked roadway connecting the waterfront with the area between First Avenue and the western end of Pike Street at the top of the bluff. Officials could see no reason why the level area behind the Leland Hotel at First and Pike could not be used, at least temporarily, as a place where farmers could park their wagons and sell their produce.

In the last week of July 1907, Councilman Revelle introduced an ordinance designating Pike Place as Seattle's public market area under terms of the 1896 ordinance. Dressed in his familiar dark, single-breasted wool suit, his brown hair brushed firmly back, he assumed the tone of a prophet as he urged adoption, not merely as a means to ease the complaints about prices, but as a way to industrialize Seattle:

> The market will in the future be the direct cause of the cultivation of immense tracts of land and cause apparently sterile fields to blossom as the rose; manufacturing industries will come as a result, because provisions must be made for the multitudes who will grow vegetables and cultivate the soil.

Before the Pike Place ordinance came to a vote in the council, Revelle found an odd but effective ally: Colonel Alden J. Blethen, the flamboyant publisher of the *Seattle Times*. Blethen was then at midpoint in his metamorphosis from Populist to reactionary, and at the height of his influence. Revelle was a persuasive advocate, Blethen a genius at attack. Together they proved invincible.

While the Pike Place ordinance was

under consideration, the Colonel's paper laid down a creeping barrage of news stories aimed at driving the commission houses out of their established positions.

The first salvo on July 31 quoted Nikola Kaumanns, identified as a visiting farm expert from Germany, as believing that "Prices are too high . . . and the brokers try to shift the blame to others' shoulders by giving the impression that their prices are such because of charges imposed by the farmers. . . . The brokers could sell their products for one third less and still make a reasonable profit."

On August 4, Dr. G. F. Abbott, the father of a Seattle city councilman, explained that he was ready to give up marketing the produce of his orchard at Coupeville on Whidbey Island because a Seattle commission merchant had offered him four cents a pound for his best grade cherries on the same day that cherries were selling for ten to twelve and a half cents in the stores.

A supporting story cited the experience of a Kent Valley farmer who told why he had given up farming some of the richest ground in the country:

I went to Seattle one day last summer and asked Western Avenue dealers what they would pay for a certain fine variety of cherry I saw on the sidewalk. They asked if I had my cherries with me. I told them I had not. They said they would give me fifteen cents a box. I went home, packed up better cherries than I saw for sale there and next day received five cents a box—not enough to pay for packing and shipping. When the cherries got there the commission men had me, and they knew it and put on the screws. The price of cherries hadn't gone down. It was just a case—a plain case—of stealing from the farmer.

I know a man who had some splendid pears. He shipped them to Western Avenue. It cost him ten cents apiece for the boxes in which the pears were packed. He paid the freight, picked the pears, and put in his time on the work. The Western Avenue commission men paid him seven cents a box for those pears. He lost three cents just on the boxes they were packed in.

We have no market. Do you wonder I went out of business? Do you wonder why this splendid farming country is being converted into a stock and dairying country? I believe the situation is unexampled in the history of the United States.

The next day, the city council passed Revelle's ordinance setting aside Pike Place as the site for a farmers' market, but the *Times* continued its cannonade. On Friday, August 8, much of the front page was given over to the inequities of the existing system. A banner headline in red proclaimed:

COMMISSION TRUST RUINS FARMERS IN WHITE RIVER VALLEY

Subheads spelled out the details: Farmers Forced Out of Business. Fruit and Vegetables Rotting in

ABOVE: *City Councilman Thomas P. Revelle led the campaign to lower food prices by eliminating the middlemen. "I knew not how the matter could be accomplished but I was determined, if it took whole of my public life, to have a market." (Photo by Prince Studio, Seattle, courtesy of Randy Revelle)*

White River Valley Because Growers Can't Get Living Prices on Western Ave., Though Cost to Seattle Consumer is Exorbitant.

Under the heading "What White River Farmers Say," a front-page box quoted producers to the effect that Western Avenue was changing one of the most fertile valleys in the Northwest into "mere stock raising country." Seattle citizens received the poorest vegetables and fruits because choice items were reserved for large-scale exporters. Seattle buyers were overcharged an average of twenty-five cents per capita daily for the sole benefit of the middlemen. The Public Market "would be the making of Seattle and its neighboring agricultural communities."

When the opening day of the Market drew thousands of visitors but less than a dozen farmers, the *Times* had explanations aplenty. Stories accused the commission men of going into the valley and buying up the day's produce before it could reach the Market, of threatening farmers with boycotts and possible violence if they tried to sell their goods at Pike Place, and of dispatching toughs to the Market to stir up trouble. Besides, there was always the rain to blame.

Whatever the merits of such charges, they helped spread word to farmer and customer alike that Pike Place was available. The following Saturday, seventy wagons went up Western Avenue, past the commission houses, and took positions by the curb. More than enough customers showed up to buy them all out.

Councilman Revelle deserves his title as Father of the Pike Place Market, but Colonel Blethen was the improbable midwife who saw the infant through its difficult birth.

ABOVE: *The planks of Western Avenue held an unregulated jumble of carts, horses, farmers, commission men, and shoppers on this summer day in 1907, just before the Public Market was created. (University of Washington Libraries, Special Collections, UW 6015)*

Chapter 2 | THE GOODWIN ERA

It rains a lot in Seattle, especially in the fall. The Market had not been in operation a week when the city council began to receive complaints that the area's exposure was indecent. The first came from the Vashon Island Fruit Producers Association, petitioning for protection against the elements:

At this time of year Vashon Island has poultry, eggs, butter and all tree fruits in great abundance. It is imperative that we have shelter from the fact that we are located from twelve to fourteen miles by water, and all fruits and other products must be shipped by boat, then hauled to the market and stored until sold . . . When a permanent market, well housed, is built, we will put 2,500 crates of berries on the market during the berry season. Even during the present season we would have nearly a carload of produce on hand every day.

The need was apparent but the answer was money. The council had none to spare. Not even Tom Revelle's enthusiasm could conjure up funds. Nor could Colonel Blethen. Frank Goodwin was the man who first put the farmers and their customers under cover.

One of six brothers born to a Scotch-Irish farm family in Kankakee, Illinois, fifty-five miles south of Chicago, Frank Goodwin was gifted, adventurous, and eccentric. He had a passion for penny stocks, he assembled his own steam-propelled automobile (which once nearly scared Theodore Roosevelt off his horse), made and lost money in District of Columbia real estate, suffered from asthma, practiced a rigorous vegetarianism, slept out of doors in his own backyard, maintained his private office next to the public restroom in a building he designed, joined the best clubs, and not only designed the Pike Place Market, but had a lasting influence on market design in other parts of the country.

He was thirty-two years old, in poor health and wan financial condition when he left Washington, D.C., in 1897 and came to Seattle intent on cashing in on the rush to the Klondike. It was his idea to invest in real estate and open a hotel, but on learning of the difficulty would-be prospectors were having in getting north

from Skagway through White Pass and Dyea Pass, he caught a ship for Skagway with the intention of enlisting some of the men wintering over at Lynn Canal and improvising a railroad across the mountains, using wooden poles for rails. That didn't work out either. Instead, he moved on to Dawson with two of his brothers, Ervin and John, staked a claim, and returned to Seattle a year later, his health restored and his poke heavy with $50,000 in dust and nuggets.

Frank, Ervin, and John formed the Goodwin Real Estate Company. It prospered. They took offices in Seattle's first steel-frame skyscraper, the Alaska Building, when it opened in 1904. Two years later, Ervin, president of the company, was featured in *Argus* as one of the instillers of the locally acclaimed "Seattle Spirit," and the firm was labeled "one of the best."

One aspect of Seattle Spirit was the search for property likely to increase in value as the result of municipal projects. Among the foresighted acquisitions of the spirited Goodwins were the Leland Hotel at the western end of Pike Street, the undeveloped land along the bluff west of Pike Place, and other land between First and Second Avenues, north of Pike.

FACING PAGE: *This classic shot of the Market was taken in 1907 looking north from the corner of Pike Place and Pike Street. (University of Washington Libraries, Special Collections, UW 443)*

ABOVE: *Frank Goodwin saw a new El Dorado in real estate bordering the Public Market and bet on a profitable return from private improvement. (Courtesy of Kerry Serl)*

On the morning the Public Market opened, Goodwin Realty ran an advertisement in the *Post-Intelligencer* urging those who patronized the Market to appreciate the value of property fronting on Pike Place:

$16,000—will buy a fractional lot on the west side, south of Pine, with over 60 feet fronting on Pike Place; Very easy terms.

Also:

$38,000—will buy 70 feet on south side of Pike Street, 120 feet west of First Avenue; lot contains 5,700 square feet.

Frank Goodwin was among those on hand to observe the Market area on opening day. What he appreciated most was the huge crowd milling in the rain. Pike Street was not too far from the traditional center of town, to the south, to draw crowds. Goodwin knew a gold mine when he saw one. Farmers and customers would want shelter. On the back of an envelope he drew a preliminary sketch for a shed to extend from the Leland Hotel north on company property along the west bank of the bluff. After consultation with his brothers, he refined the plan, dividing the area into seventy-six stalls that they decided could be rented at rates varying from four to twenty-five dollars a month. Farmers and gardeners marketing their own produce would be given first priority as tenants.

Work started immediately. By November 30, 1907, the building was complete, every stall rented. Wagner's forty-piece band, mounted on a low platform decorated with flowers and bunting, stirred the crowd with Sousa marches. There were cheers when Councilman Tom Revelle, got up in top hat and tails, approached the podium; more cheers when a farmer thrust in his hands a huge pumpkin; and still more when he set it down by the speaker's stand, placed his silk hat on it, and with political resonance addressed the assemblage:

The public market is of the greatest possible moment to the householders of Seattle, and it is because they were impressed with its value to the community, especially to the workers of the community, that so many of them are here today. This is a glorious and auspicious occasion, but it is only the beginning of what will be the finest market system in the world . . .

Some months ago, in Seattle, the question of how the average man was to get a sufficient supply of vegetables at a price within his means became a serious one. He was the victim of organized greed and, in spite of the fact that there was and is an abundance of all good things in the country, his children were deprived of vegetables and fruit. Wages were, and are, good; but no matter how liberal an employer might be, he could not

FACING PAGE, ABOVE: *Frank Goodwin, a self-taught architect, sketched on the back of an envelope his plans for a building extending north along Pike Place from the Leland Hotel. It needed underpinning, which became the labyrinthine substructure of the Market. An unknown photographer took this picture from Western Avenue in 1912. (City of Seattle)*

FACING PAGE, BELOW: *The Market had assumed a more familiar configuration in 1909 when this picture was taken. Goodwin's arcade extends north from the Leland Hotel. The automobile has appeared to contest right-of-way with the wagons at the eternally congested Pike Street–Pike Place bend. Merchants had discovered the appeal of awnings. (University of Washington Libraries, Special Collections, SEA 469)*

in those days pay money enough without going into bankruptcy to give his men's families a reasonable quantity of vegetables.

I saw this condition and it appealed to me, and I felt that I must do something to obtain a public market that would make conditions as they then existed impossible of perpetuation. I knew not how the matter could be accomplished, but I was determined if it took the whole of my public life to have a market; and this, you see, with the assistance of loyal citizens of all shades of political opinion, is the result.

The benefits have already proved to be immeasurable. Food products are reduced in cost. The man who could not feed his family properly a few months ago can give them more

to eat, even if he has to work for less wages. The Market will in the future be the direct cause of the cultivation of immense tracts of land and cause apparently sterile fields to blossom as the rose; manufacturing industries will come as a result, because provi-

FACING PAGE, ABOVE: *Frank Goodwin's private development led the city to undertake the construction of adjoining arcades to offer shelter to farmers and their customers. Revelle sponsored the ordinance.* (Seattle Times, *October 18, 1910*)

ABOVE AND FACING PAGE, BELOW: *Coucilman Tom Revelle predicted that lowering the cost of food would lead not only to development of the Market itself, but to "cultivation of immense tracks of land and would cause apparently sterile fields to blossom as the rose." (Above: State Library Collection, Washington State Archives; Facing page, below: Washington State Historical Society, Asahel Curtis, 20010)*

sion must be made for the multitudes who will grow vegetables and cultivate the soil.

The only trade that will not be benefited by the Market is the trade of graft. Every other trade will receive an immense impetus and the whole city, in fact the entire Puget Sound country, will reap a rich harvest from this enterprise. It is here to stay and there is no influence, no power, no combination and no set of either political or commercial grafters that will destroy it.

This market is yours. I dedicate it to you, and may it prove a benefit to you and your children. It is for you to defend, to protect and to uphold, and it is for you to see that those who occupy it treat you fairly; that no extortion be permitted and that the purpose for which it was created be religiously adhered to. This is one of the greatest days in the history of Seattle, but it is only a beginning for soon this city will have one of the greatest markets in the world.

The assembled farmers and consumers cheered, the band struck up another march, and the crowd dispersed to shop at stalls filled with late fall produce. Thus was proclaimed the de facto marriage of the private and public markets. Both parties to the union grew in patronage and popularity, but their relationship, though meaningful, was not harmonious for long.

CITY ESTABLISHES PUBLIC MARKET

Councilman Revelle's bill appropriating $10,000 for market stalls in Pike Place passed the city council. Plans are being perfected by the building inspector's department, and it is expected that the stalls will be ready for occupancy early in December.

This action of the council doubtless permanently establishes the market in Pike Place, since there is adequate opportunity in Pike Place to enlarge the market to meet the city's future needs.

The members of the finance committee of the council gave no encouragement to the Lindeberg proposal to establish a public market at Westlake, believing it would be harmful to the city's own market at Pike Place, and that it would be folly to establish another market so close, since one or the other would most likely fail.

The original ordinance creating a public market set the hours of operation as 5 A.M. to noon, Monday through Saturday, and made the Department of Streets responsible for supervision of the facility. Within weeks, this was amended. Ordinance 317187 let the Market remain open until 9 A.M. on Saturdays. It also called in the cops: the police department was required to have at least one officer in attendance during marketing hours. He was to assign stall space to the farmers on the basis of first come, first served; to enforce rules, the most important being that space on the planked street be assigned only to those who had raised, produced, or manufactured the goods offered for sale; and to maintain order.

The street market stretched northward as Seattle's population continued to swell. By August 1911, the double row of stalls extended from Pike to Stewart Street. Demand was so great that the stall lines, which ordinance required to be "plainly marked upon curb, sidewalk, or street," were narrowed to between four and five feet from the previous seven to eight feet. A canopy was erected over the stalls on the west side and they became known as "the dry row," coveted by producers whose goods would not benefit from watering. A rent of twenty cents a day was imposed, wet or dry.

The city council created the offices of Market Inspector (changed in 1912 to

BE LOYAL

— TO —

SEATTLE'S FIRST

PUBLIC MARKET

PIKE PLACE

is the only CITY public market; all others are private and not public markets.

The city has officers here to control and inspect for your protection all foods sold.

Your friends here were the first who had the nerve to start a public market and assail the food trust and bring relief to you.

Our big business has excited the envy of certain "big private interests" at Westlake who seek to grab the fruits of our toil. Tell them to start some other new industry instead for Seattle's benefit.

Big cities are able to support but one central market.

Seattle had better have one good, big, successful market than to have two inferior, half dead markets so close together and struggling to live on the same trade which supports but one now at

PIKE PLACE

Market Master), Assistant Market Inspector, and Janitor. The Market Master was put in charge of assigning the stalls and collecting the fees. John Winship, the first Market Master, began the practice of allocating stalls by lottery. Two rolls of tickets were printed daily, each bearing the number of a stall. The numbers were not in numerical order. One roll was for the wet row, the other for the "inside market," or dry row. About 1:30 every day, the Market Master walked down the line of farmers, giving the top ticket to each man as he came to him. The farmer paid his fee and kept the ticket as title to that number stall on the following morning.

In passing out tickets, Winship at first had Japanese farmers draw from the odd-numbered roll, all others from the even-numbered. The Japanese soon protested this segregation. At the time, more than half the vendors on an average day were Japanese. If they drew from only one set of numbers, their chance of getting a low-numbered stall at the Pike Street end of the Market where pedestrian traffic was heaviest was somewhat decreased. Winship saw the logic of their complaint and made the draw completely random.

Customers sometimes complained. Some vendors, usually one-visit sharpshooters out for a quick kill, weighed down potato bags and other containers of heavy produce with sand or gravel, or put wadded paper in the bottom of fruit cartons. Others yielded to the temptation of displaying choice specimens but filling the bags with spoiled or unripe fruit and vegetables. Men weighing meat and poultry, according to one observer, were known to "let their hands linger lovingly

FACING PAGE: *The popularity of the Pike Place Public Market led to the threat of rival establishments. Goodwin defended his turn with advertising.*

RIGHT: *Developers used the existence of the Market to promote farmlands east of Lake Washington. The advertisement about booming Kirkland appeared in the* Seattle Times *in 1910.*

BELOW: *The $10,000 arcade of stalls was ready for occupancy by early 1911. Some vendors still provided umbrellas, and merchants provided them in return for free advertisements. (University of Washington Libraries, Special Collections, UW 4763)*

KIRKLAND'S CLOSE TO MARKET

Within easy driving distance. Whatever you raise you can sell at top-notch prices—and it all goes into your own pocket. No freight to pay. No commission or middlemen to take the bulk of your profits. You sell direct to the consumer. You get the money, not the other fellow who fattens on the producer's industry. This, because

Kirkland Homesteads Are Within 30 Minutes of Seattle

With a direct ferry. When you raise $500 to $1,500 an acre—as you can on this rich soil—you get the whole proceeds yourself. It won't take long to figure your profits when you consider that you can buy this land at

$150 Up Per Acre on Your Own Terms

If you don't delay until the few remaining tracts are gone. Nearest acreage to Seattle and at half to quarter price asked much farther away. Time and distance saved mean money earned. Don't go further and fare worse.

Make the Most of This Today

Take Madison cars to Madison Park and then Kirkland ferry or Anderson boats to office on wharf at Kirkland.
All offices open evenings.

BURKE & FARRAR
OWNERS
405-409 NEW YORK BLOCK
Capital and Surplus $1,000,000

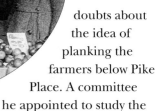

on the cut, so that for every pound of meat they sell, a customer frequently pays for a quarter pound or more of hand."

The Market Master prowled the Market, on the alert for such tricks. Signs were posted warning the public what to look out for. If Winship caught anyone cheating, or if a farmer was the subject of frequent complaints, he was denied stall space.

The farmers had their own complaints. They thought the twenty cents a day stall charge was too high: it was cut to a dime. Vendors who came to Seattle on steamers or brought their produce in their own small boats hated the climb up the bluff. They wanted the city to run a conveyor belt between the wharf and the Market. Valley farmers and island farmers alike complained of overcrowding. More stalls were needed.

When the city failed to act on the latter complaints, the farmers used the new amendment to the state constitution that permitted the citizenry to initiate legislation. They circulated an initiative petition calling for a $150,000 bond issue to provide funds to dig an 800-foot tunnel under Pike Place to provide space for 400 more stalls. This underground market was to be linked by conveyor belt to the waterfront.

Reform Mayor George Cotterill was an engineer. Though no foe of the farmer or of the initiative process, he had doubts about the idea of planking the farmers below Pike Place. A committee he appointed to study the proposal reported that the subterranean market would be hard to enter, hard to ventilate, hard to keep sanitary, and more expensive to create than the sponsors claimed.

Cotterill had an alternative ordinance drawn. It provided that the central forty-two feet of Pike Place would be paved for traffic and twelve feet on each side would be improved for wagon stalls or market tables, under shelter. Arcaded sidewalks fifteen feet wide would be built on each side of Pike Place. A second public market area would be designated for development on Westlake. The total cost would be $25,000.

Both initiatives went to the voters on March 13, 1913. The farmers' initiative was rejected; the Mayor's passed easily. Work on the public arcades began at once.

Meanwhile, Frank Goodwin had been roaming Pike Place looking at the land with an eye ever more focused on the needs and complexities of a market. He had no formal training in architecture, this self-trained handyman and promoter, but he was practical, inventive, widely read, and passionate about vegetables and fresh air. He slept out of doors on a platform under a tree overlooking Lake Washington at his summer home in the Hunts Point district. Most days he walked

to the Market from his Seattle home and returned with shopping bags full of fresh vegetables. Eschewing any "flesh food," as he called it, he insisted on at least two legumes for his evening meal. He was fond of freshly ground horseradish and garlic, and he conscientiously dipped his celery in olive oil. He believed that the fresher the food, the greater its nutritional value, and his desire to have produce sold quickly influenced his market designs.

The sketches he made for the development of the private property the Goodwin brothers and their associates owned alongside the Pike Place Public Market reflected his idiosyncratic personal habits and the theories he was developing about public markets in general, theories later quoted in a book, *Markets: Public and Private*, by his nephew and acolyte Arthur Goodwin:

Store Frontage: A common mistake in the design of a market is that of devoting the choice store frontage to a series of stores, and placing the market proper in the rear of the building.

Simple Design: It should not present too costly an appearance or be so decorative in ornamentation that it would have a tendency to discourage trade among patrons who are drawn to the market because of the necessity of saving on the purchase of foods.

Aesthetics: Inasmuch as ninety percent of the market patrons are women, it is evident that the pleasing display of flowers, shrubs and plants will make a strong appeal to them.

To the architect: Utility and economy rather than ornamental and costly construction should be the major objective . . .

These ideas are reflected in the buildings the Goodwins erected around Pike Place, but before they could be made manifest, new financial arrangements were necessary. The Public Market &

FACING PAGE: *Scales were a frequent source of suspicion and complaint. The Market Master and men from the City Department of Weights made periodic checks and Frank Goodwin supplied free scales on which customers could check weights for themselves. A stall on the dry row. (City of Seattle)*

ABOVE: *An inspector checking on a scale in the wet row. (Seattle Department of Weights and Measures)*

Department Store Company, a private entity, was created in 1910 to develop and manage the Goodwin Real Estate Company's holdings in the Pike Place area. The new company included most of those involved in the original real estate venture—the three Goodwins, David Bell Fairley, and R. E. B. Smith. Frank Goodwin was president.

Their first work, in 1911, was to finish the original building in the triangular area north of the Leland Hotel. The improvements embodied Frank Goodwin's concept of openness, plainness, and ease of circulation, but they were only a piece in his larger vision of a central building that would anchor the entire district.

"Our purpose," he said, "is to enlarge and improve the old building occupying all of the ground on the northwest corner of Pike Street and Pike Place to an expanded three or four-story market structure. A feature of the new plans is a proposal that the Pike Place frontage of the building shall be set back ten feet from the sidewalk. In the arcade between the store front and the sidewalk will be selling space from which farmers can sell their produce."

In a way, the proposed four-story market answered the demands of the farmers' initiative of 1913. Goodwin's concept, however, was not an underground emporium beneath Pike Place, but a 240-foot long building hung on the face of the Pike Place bluff, descending story by story to Western Avenue, with its western windows opening to vistas of Elliott Bay, Puget Sound, and the Olympic Mountains.

In 1914, Goodwin's dream took its labyrinthine shape. The addition, extending westward and downward, included on its main floor more space for merchants, refrigerators, and balcony sections for the already-established Manning's Restaurant (now Lowell's) and St. Germain's Bread. Thirteen new stalls and farmers' tables were embedded in the lower mezzanine. Then came the lower market floor with room for a printing plant, public toilet, office, restaurant, creamery, butcher shop, and grain market. The two bottom floors were laid out for storage of

BELOW: *The first of many proposals to transform the Market into something grandiose was put forward in 1913. It was rejected by the voters. (City of Seattle)*

poultry, meat, fruit, and grains. One area in Goodwin's design was enigmatically labeled "room with water under floor."

The addition included more than one hundred shop spaces, most of them rectangular. It was of mill construction—structural steel and wooden beams. Railings were of round steel with stock wood bannisters. There was little ornamentation except for a pair of modified Doric columns at the Pike and Pike Place entrance, ornamental capitals with festoons of fruit throughout the interior arcade, and clusters of seventy-five-watt bulbs on the ceiling. The market was designed to emphasize the product, not the architect. Goodwin didn't put his name on a cornerstone; indeed, he didn't even put in a cornerstone.

In 1916, the Goodwins obtained a lease on the Bartell Building at the corner of First Avenue and Pike Street. Frank renamed it the Economy Market, redesigned the space to hold sixty-five stalls and stores, plus an area for wholesaling sugar, and a space later converted to a dime-a-dance ballroom. Frank let himself go a bit on decor for the Economy—more Doric columns than in the main market, more plaster garlands of fruit and flowers, more clusters of lights, some frescoes, and even an electric sign over the entrance.

Even so, simplicity remained Frank Goodwin's style. He took for his office a cubicle alongside the public toilets in the lower market. Subject to flood when the plumbing jammed, his headquarters was neither well-ventilated or well-lighted—odd for a man with a fresh air fetish. But it was from this cavern barely large enough to accommodate two desks and two chairs that Frank Goodwin, with the aid of his nephew Arthur, directed the major segment of the privately owned market facilities in the Pike Place area.

Arthur Goodwin was the son of

ABOVE: *When the Goodwins leased the Bartell Building in 1916, Frank redesigned it into the Economy Market recognizable today. The picture is dated 1916 in a Goodwin promotion pamphlet, but the absence of wagons indicates it was taken later. (City of Seattle)*

Joseph Henry Goodwin, one of the brothers who had not rushed west from Kankakee during the Klondike excitement. Instead, Joseph had rushed east to New York, where he combined the careers of accountant, author of guidebooks on business practices, and Shakespearean actor and producer. The Manhattan apartment in which Arthur was reared included a large room with a small stage on which his father auditioned would-be interpreters of the Bard.

As a youth, Arthur mastered the intricacies of both double-entry bookkeeping and Elizabethan cadence. He painted in oil, developed glass plate photographs in his own darkroom, and, as he put it, practiced "legerdemain and prestidigitation," none of them profitably. In 1907, when Arthur was twenty, his Seattle uncles wrote suggesting he come and grow up with their city and their firm. The young man went west and, after an apprenticeship of eight years, Arthur Goodwin became assistant manager of the Public Market & Department Store Company.

A slight, dapper young man of twenty-eight, Arthur was a compulsive record-keeper, an adder-up and subtracter-from who earned a reputation as a walking balance sheet and unquenchable absorber

of information. He served as his uncle's antennae on Market activities. Arthur stood around listening so much to vendors and their customers that he learned to speak Japanese and Italian and to give dialect imitations in Swedish, German, and polyglot.

Among his duties was the task of seeing that customers were fairly treated. When the Market Master reported complaints against vendors renting space from the Public Market & Department Store Company, Arthur recorded the details in a small black book and called in the tenant to discuss the charges. He took the matter seriously. In an article for the Toledo Scale Company magazine, he declared that "the success of the operator of markets depends upon the success of the merchants. . . . It is incumbent upon the operators to prescribe such regulations as will preclude failure from loose methods, unsatisfactory service or antiquated systems." Though the first complaint usually resulted in a warning, a second usually meant the tenant was evicted.

Arthur Goodwin recorded an encounter with a fruit peddler bearing the wonderful name of Mrs. Blunder. She entered his office wiping her hands on a well-stained apron, plunked broadly into the chair in front of his desk, and eyed Arthur sternly.

"People tell me that you've been selling them what they think is fresh produce," he told her. "When they get home they find they have a bag half-full of rotten fruit. What have you to say?"

Mrs. Blunder gasped, covered her face with fruit-stained hands, but kept her fingers parted enough so she could study her accuser: "I'm so honest," she assured him, "that if I try to put a rotten banana in a bag my hand shakes so bad I can't get it in." This profession of good result if not

good intent won her a second chance, but somehow Mrs. Blunder was able to subdue her qualms. With steady hand she continued to load enough overage fruit into customers' bags to win disqualification from market space.

The relationship between Frank and Arthur was more that of father and son, or ruler and heir-apparent, than uncle and nephew. They operated the Market complex with familial informality. Most mornings Arthur dropped by his uncle's place on his way to work. Frank would produce a day's memos, most of them written on old envelopes. They covered everything from the desirability of locating new marketplaces near established streetcar stops to ways of preventing bruises on peaches. Before Arthur left, they would have agreed on what most needed to be done during the day.

Frank would come to the office (some called it the Privy Councilchamber) in midmorning. After checking the mail and dealing with any policy matters that might have arisen, he would get on the phone to his stockbroker. Frugal in personal habits and simple in his architectural taste,

Frank was a gaudy plunger in speculation. He invested in oil wells, founded a petroleum company, bought grape lands in the Columbia River Basin half a century too soon, accumulated alleged oyster beds in the rockless Nisqually delta, and snapped up penny stocks, most of which came to be valued not in millions but in mills. Proceeds from the Market made such ventures less painful. All the while, Frank kept a thoughtful eye on the Market and Arthur. He liked what he saw and eventually sold the business to his nephew.

FACING PAGE: *In redesigning the Economy Market, Frank combined Doric columns with Edison lighting. (University of Washington Libraries, Special Collections, photo by Mary Randlett, Mary Randlett collection.)*

ABOVE: *By 1913, when Asahel Curtis took this picture for A. J. Fisken, the Market had assumed the configuration familiar today, with the Corner Market and Sanitary Market buildings on the east side of Pike Place, the Goodwin labyrinth and the stalls on the west side. The streets were still boarded, and the automobiles were nearly as numerous as the delivery wagons. (Washington State Historical Society, photo by Asahel Curtis, 27125)*

Chapter 3 | THE MARKET IN FLOWER

Approaching its tenth anniversary in 1917, the Market was an established institution, a recognized, even cherished, part of community life. At least a third of Seattle's population had been born or had immigrated to the town after the Market was created. For them, Pike Place was a permanent part of the furniture of their lives.

The prospect as one approached Pike Place differed little in outline from today's Market, aside from the notable absence today of stall space on the street itself. The Corner Market Building, created in 1912 from a design by the architectural firm of Thomas & Grainger, stood at the northwest corner of Pike and First Avenue, across from the Economy

Market. North from the Corner Market was the Sanitary Public Market, so called (some say) because horses were not allowed within its confines. Across Pike Place sprawled the intriguing maze of Goodwins' Main Market Building. Down each side of Pike Place, reaching now as far as Virginia Street, were the tables and stalls rented daily by the city to those selling their own produce.

Few customers made distinction between farmers who rented municipally owned space and middlemen who leased stalls in privately owned buildings. It is doubtful that many realized the buildings weren't public property. What drew patrons to the Market were low prices, a variety of fresh foods, and the ambience of an occidental bazaar. Pike Place was a hive of activity, where Horseradish Jerry ground roots into pungent, self-advertising relish; where Robert Maddox told tales of his days in the Klondike as he twisted twine and wove nets which became sturdy shopping bags, pausing in his work from time to time to feel the words of Dickens or Shakespeare in one of the volumes of braille stacked beside him; where newsboys hawked the pink-covered *Seattle Star* or the chaos of red headlines in Second-Coming type that was characteristic of the *Seattle Times*. You could find almost anything at the Market, from violets to mastadon tusks, sometimes truffles, and always salmon (though the price was no longer a standard two bits a fish).

On Saturdays ill-clad youngsters from an orphanage in Des Moines gave horn and drum concerts on the sidewalk in front of a flower stall under the arcade, the bright flowers contrasting with the kids' threadbare clothing, a tin can on the cement indicating what the sympathetic might do to make the children bloom.

The Three Girls Bakery, which had occupied a spot in the Corner Market since the building opened for business, was now officially known as the Rotary Bakery, though popularly referred to as "The Gals." Crowds gathered to watch its automatic doughnut caster, Seattle's first, pop sixty gobs of dough a minute from a cone into a coiled trough steaming with hot oil. There they sputtered and browned until flipped by an automatic hand; they cooked a bit more, then slid out, each a golden temptation of starch and cholesterol. Farm kids thought it was like watching hens lay boiled eggs, and parents soon learned that the doughnut machine could baby-

---

FACING PAGE: *The intersection of First Avenue and Pike Street was one of Seattle's busiest corners. One of four streetcar riders passed it, one in eight disembarked or boarded a car here. Built in 1912, the Corner Market with its repeated arches became one of the city's most familiar landmarks. (Washington State Historical Society, photo by Ashael Curtis, 23706)*

ABOVE: *Though the automobile was becoming important as a means of family transportation, most farmers still brought their goods in wagons. This picture, looking north up Pike Place, was taken on May 1, 1912. (Photo by Asahel Curtis, Special Collections, University of Washington Libraries, A Curtis, 23588)*

sit their spellbound children while they shopped in unencumbered leisure.

There were other amenities special to the Market area. Liberty Theater, across First Avenue, hired an attendant to watch over laden market baskets while their owners went to the nickel matinee. Lightning, a big white tomcat, protected the produce from pigeons, rats, and small dogs.

Tuesday was the traditional day off for servants in Seattle homes. The Market soon became a focal point for off-duty maids, many of them daughters of Scandinavian, Italian, or Japanese families working farms up the valley or on the islands. The girls promenaded the passageways to see and be seen, or lingered over hot chocolate on the balcony at Manning's, watching the little ships of the inland sea that might be bringing kin or boyfriends to town.

The mosquito fleet, as Seattle residents called the vessels that never ventured onto the open ocean, was in decline, a victim of the automobile that offered the commuter more flexibility. Ferries were challenging the passenger-steamers for customers, but though the half-century in which the Sound was western Washington's best highway was drawing to a close, the little ships still brought much produce and many customers to Seattle.

The weekly or biweekly trip to market was an outing for islanders, a break in the isolation on a small farm beyond electricity, beyond telephone, beyond commercial entertainment. Sometimes whole families made the trip, but often go-to-market day provided the opportunity for women to have a day in town while their husbands looked after the children and the farm.

When the boat whistled its approach, the farmers or their wives would gather on the dock, bringing chickens dressed and wrapped in cheesecloth; butter molded into rose patterns, wrapped in butter-paper, and packed in wooden boxes; eggs nestled in straw baskets; root vegetables in burlap sacks; milk in galvanized cans; crates of fruit; bundles of rhubarb.

The crew, sometimes even the captain, helped the women tote goods up the gangplank and store them on the forward deck where cargo that did not require longshoring was carried free of charge. Sometimes a goat or sheep or calf would be tethered to the rail. The farmwomen usually had in their baskets jugs of coffee, loaves of that morning's bread, still steaming, rich country butter, and cookies or pies. These were shared

with fellow passengers and the crew. A farm girl could win a reputation among young crewmen as a desirable preparer of provender. Mixed with the sounds of ship and sea and gulls were conversations in Norwegian and Swedish, Finnish, German, Italian, Serbo-Croatian and Slovene, Tagalog, too, Chinese and Japanese, even in English. Old settlers showed off their mastery of the Chinook jargon.

When the boat tied up at Seattle, some islanders would carry their produce up the ramp and steps that the city had

---

FACING PAGE: *Horseradish Jerry was a familiar sight in the Market for nearly twenty years. He ground the roots on the spot, and the aroma of the pungent relish helped advertise his product. (City of Seattle)*

BELOW: *The Three Girls Bakery, though not always doing business at the same old stand, has been around the Market since World War I. It still features Brenner's bread. (University of Washington Libraries, Special Collections, Todd, 12304)*

built across the tracks from waterfront to market. If the load was too heavy, they'd hire a cart. George Thompson, a favorite deliveryman, gloried in his reputation for never having broken an egg.

Because most steamers arrived no earlier than 10 A.M., the island farmers were at a disadvantage in competing for customers in the early hours when most hotel and restaurant purchases were made. Some came on the late Friday runs and stayed overnight. The Hotel Dix, a large wooden building on the hillside north of the Market, offered special rates for regular visitors: two bits a night, beds with fresh sheets, and an early morning call-up so the islanders could get to their

stalls as early as the valley folk who came by wagon.

Even so, it was difficult to get ahead of the valley farmers. First comers were on hand in the deep darkness of 4 A.M. and most were there by 7 A.M., even if they paused on their inbound trek to balance their load by swapping produce with those who grew other crops. When they arrived, some farmers simply unloaded

ABOVE: *The Liberty Theater, across First Avenue from the Pike Place Market, catered to shoppers by hiring a watchman to guard grocery bags too bulky to be taken into the movie. Sometimes he had to guard meat and fish from Lightning, the theater cat. (State Library Collection, Washington State Archives)*

their goods and stalled their horses in livery stables, but competition introduced refinements. Farmers accustomed to the county and state fairs of the Midwest began to arrange their produce in patterns. Customers were saluted by mosaics: an American eagle in beets, the Smith Tower in celery, a butterfly in rutabagas and turnips. Then the Japanese offered embellishments on a smaller scale: their radishes and turnips became roses. Scandinavians even experimented with radishes on lutefisk! Such sharing of folk art evolved into a cosmopolitanism deplored by ethnic purists but accepted by the community that came to relish Scots and Serbs sculpturing root crops into table corsages.

Between seven and eight o'clock each morning, drummers for assorted paper products circulated through the Market with brown bags. Vendors who purchased a day's supply were rewarded by display bags that were then painted with that day's price of each vegetable offered. One Japanese distributor created price tags in the broad-brush *sumi* tradition, producing art worthy of framing.

The variety of ethnic backgrounds among the farmer-vendors seemed to have calmed rather than exacerbated racial trouble. Exchanges of epithets and gestures were usually *pro forma*, but even when intended as deadly insult might miss the mark between an Italian and a Japanese whose cultures did not share the significance of hand clapping flexor muscle or thumb flipping out between front teeth.

Even the outbreak of war in Europe in 1914 failed to stir nationalist antagonisms in the Market. Smith's English Bakery fired no salvos across the aisle at the Kiaska German Delicatessen. Great Britain might proclaim Egypt its protectorate to the disadvantage of

Turkey and the Central Powers, but the Ovaita Fish Company saw no need to take reprisals against the Egyptian Hama Cone people. "World wars may and do rage but man must eat," observed a philosophic reporter for the *Seattle Star*. "Wars can and do swing like the pendulum of doom, but the Sunday roast is not to be neglected."

The American entry into the conflict on April 6, 1917, did, however, bring changes. The state armory, only a block north of the Market on Western Avenue, resounded to shouts of command and the thud of boots on the wooden floor as National Guardsmen drilled in preparation for the mud and trenches of the Western Front. As sons and husbands went into uniform or left in pursuit of assembly-line pay, more and more women worked the Market stalls.

Food production became part of the war effort and thrifty shopping a mark of patriotism. It was fashionable for well-to-do women to do their own shopping, though few could match the grand style of Mrs. Anderson, wife of the owner of the Phoenix Lumber Company, who descended from Capitol Hill in a large coach drawn by matched horses with a plump coachman in the driver's seat, a footman at the sideboard, and an accompanying retinue of Dalmatian coach dogs. The footman would help her from the coach and accompany her as she swept through the Market, pointing out the vegetables and meats that struck her fancy. Another dowager always came in a black limousine with a black chauffeur.

Frank Goodwin sometimes arrived for his hours in the office in the steam-propelled auto he had designed and assembled himself. It had big, thin tires, tufted leather upholstery, and brass ornamentation that scooped around from front to back like the trim on a carriage. Small boys cheered when it puffed past on the plank streets.

Those with leisure and money tended to shop in midmorning when the selection was still good. The poor and thrifty came by streetcar or on foot near closing time when farmers unloaded produce at bargain rates rather than cart it back home. Kids from poor families fished for discards in the water barrels that were used for washing vegetables while their mothers haggled for bargains. Late in the day, most vendors gave a baker's dozen on all purchases, tossing in "one for the baby." Fish heads and tails were given "for the cat," though they might well wind up in the soup. Scrapings of cheese could be gathered for sandwiches or seasoning.

The Market had become important in preventing profiteering on food. Prices charged by independent farmers at their stalls came to be quoted as the going daily rate around town and put limits on what the commission houses could demand. When there was a sudden rise in the cost of fish, with salmon going for as much as twenty-five cents a pound, the State Fisheries Commission turned over to the city government the carcasses of hatchery salmon which had been killed for their eggs and sperm. Seattle established the municipally owned City Fish Market in Pike Place and competition brought the salmon price down to ten cents a pound within weeks. (The city gave up its role as fishmonger and price-fixer after the war.)

September was always the busiest month of the year at the Market, and in 1917, 5,217 farmers rented stalls, though most were there only one or two days. Overcrowding along Pike Place led to the submission of an initiative proposing a $600,000 expansion. The Seattle Municipal League undertook a study which reported that the city, with its estimated population of 340,000, was served by 550 grocery stores, 160 butcher shops, 35 delicatessens, and 12 market buildings, including the Corner Market, Sanitary Market, Pike Place, and Economy Market in the Pike complex. The League argued that Seattle had more market space per capita than any other American community and recommended against approval of the bond issue.

Even the sympathetic *Seattle Times* ran stories indicating that the Market as it was should be considered a garden of earthly delights, in scant need of improvement. "The fragrance of fresh candy bursts forth from one store, is wafted along the corridors, is vanquished by another odor, of fresh coffee, which, all conquering, takes possession of fifty yards in either direction . . . Refrigerators disgorge huge flanks of

FACING PAGE: *The steamer* Hyak, *built in Portland in 1909, was a frequent caller in Seattle for the next thirty years. One of the most rakish vessels in the mosquito fleet, she brought passengers and produce from many of the saltwater communities until automobiles, bridges, and ferries changed the pattern of traffic. (Historical Society of Seattle and King County, Joe Williamson Collection)*

BELOW: *After the adoption of state prohibition in 1914, fruit juices were much in demand. Some vendors warned that they could be fermented. (City of Seattle, photo by I. Anderson)*

meat, with which aproned gladiators will gravely wrestle forthwith."

Such redolent prose, along with the Municipal League's stark statistics, contributed to the defeat of the proposed bond issue at the polls. Also rejected were measures to finance light and water system improvements. The voters' minds were not on civic amenities but on victory in Europe.

The German surrender on November 11, 1918, marked the end of this period of shared national purpose. Class and ethnic rivalries, long suppressed, came quickly to the surface after the end of the war to make the world safe for democracy. The immediate problem of democratic life in Seattle centered on the shipyards. They had been the major source of the city's industrial expansion during the war years, and of union expansion as well. When shipyard workers struck to preserve their wartime gains, other unions sympathetic to their cause called a general strike.

A General Strike Committee representing all the city's unions set February 6, 1919, as the day when the town's entire work force except those vital to health and safety would hit the bricks. On

Tuesday, February 4, the *Union Record*, the only daily newspaper published in the United States by organized labor (with its offices at 1915 First Avenue, overlooking the Market), ran perhaps the most famous and controversial editorial in Seattle's history. Written by Anna Louise Strong, a rebellious pacifist whose anti-war activities had led to her recall from the Seattle school board, it sounded to some like a call for revolution. It began:

> THURSDAY AT 10 A.M.
> There will be many cheering, and there will be some who fear. Both these emotions are useful, but not too much of either. We are undertaking the most tremendous movement ever made by Labor in this country, a move which will lead
> NO ONE KNOWS WHERE

Strong's essay concluded in the same tone:

> Labor will not only shut down the industries, but Labor will reopen, under the management of the appropriate trades, such activities as are needed to preserve public health and public peace. If the strike continues, Labor may feel led to avoid public suffering by reopening more and more activities, UNDER ITS OWN MANAGEMENT. And this is why we say we are starting on a road that leads
> NO ONE KNOWS WHERE!

The next day there was a run on the Market as panicky buyers laid in stocks of food. Such fresh vegetables as were available in February were swept from the stalls by midmorning. Before evening, most stores reported their stocks of staples gone. On Thursday, the day scheduled for the strike, few farmers and almost no customers came to the Market.

The general strike began at 10 A.M. when whistles sounded in the mills and on the ships at the docks. Industrial and trade activity stopped at once. Banks

FACING PAGE: *A Japanese bag salesman started the practice of painting produce prices on brown bags in* sumi *style. (Washington State Historical Society, photo by Asahel Curtis, 1926, 50875)*

TOP: *The State Armory took on new significance with the U.S. declaration of war on Germany. (University of Washington Libraries, Special Collections, SEA 588)*

ABOVE: *Some have been stolen and some have been dismantled, but City Fish has always had a salmon sign. (Photo by Mary Randlett)*

locked their doors. Schools let out. Conductors took streetcars back to the barn or left them standing on the tracks. Backshop men put tarpaulins over the printing presses and linotype operators let the lead cool in the pots. Elevator boys shut the gates on their lifts. Maids stopped making the hotel beds. The few farmers who had brought produce to the Market reloaded their carts and fled toward their farms. Clerks left the counters in the covered Market, now empty and silent.

Top: *Newlyweds in 1916 strike formal poses in front of the owner's stall. The best man partially obscures a sign that advises, "You can visit my Stall, But not my Wife." (State Library Collection, Washington State Archives)*

Above: *The Seattle Star put national and Market news in interesting perspective.*

The only activity was at the nearby armory which served as command center for 1,500 troops trucked in that morning from Camp Lewis, and at the *Union Record* office, where men identified by armbands as Labor Guards stood watch to protect the newspaper against an attack by vigilantes who never arrived.

There was no violence, but for the next five days the Market was all but deserted, the longest period of inactivity in its history. After five days, the strike petered out. Labor and its sympathizers had demonstrated that they could shut down the town, but not that they knew what to do with a shut-down town. Management had refused to yield to the demands of the shipyard workers, but even paying reduced wages was unable to keep the yards in operation. Manufacturing and the industrial work force subsided together. The union movement had been blunted, but the problem of achieving equitable economic relationships remained unsolved. The traditional divisions and antagonisms remained in town and in the Market.

When City Councilman T. H. Bolton introduced an ordinance calling for expansion of the Market in a plan similar to that turned down by the voters in 1917, a spokesman for the Seattle Producers Association objected that it would be of most benefit "to a few Japanese truck gardeners from the White River, Snohomish and Skagit valleys," who, he argued, "produce less than five percent of the farm products consumed in the city."

Bolton's ordinance got nowhere.

ABOVE: *Girls in the Camp Hotel look down on a cortege forming in front of the Butterworth Mortuary at 1921 First Avenue. (Seattle Public Library)*

ABOVE, LEFT: The Union Record, *the only daily newspaper published by organized labor, converted a second-floor storage space on First Avenue into a combined city room and business office. Here Anna Louise Strong wrote Seattle's most famous editorial. (Courtesy of Mrs. Lloyd Graves)*

LEFT: *When expansion of the Market facilities was proposed after World War I, some argued that improvements would mostly benefit "a few Japanese truck gardeners from the White River, Snohomish and Skagit valleys." (Photo by Frank Natsuhara)*

48313
SAMEL CURTIS

Chapter 4 | Whose Market Is It, Anyway?

In 1919, Willard Soames a lank, dour young man of
English extraction, returned to the family farm north of
Seattle. That same year the Street Department paved Elliott
Way and Frank Goodwin began thinking of expanding the
privately owned Pike Place Market. These disparate events
were key elements in a decade-long contest over the purpose, survival, and control of the Market.

Willard Soames grew up on a 160-acre farm. His family
grew truck, ran a small dairy, and raised chickens. As a boy
he often helped dress out fryers and stewing hens (a messy,
not especially rewarding business), then accompanied his
father to a stall in the dry row. When the great shipyard

boom began in 1916, Willard bolted to the big city. He apprenticed as a riveter and for two years spent days and sometimes nights crawling around between decks of liberty ship hulls, sewing plates together with steel pins. This was hard on the ears, hard on the knees, hard on the elbows and kidneys, but profitable. Willard might have kept at it, but after victory, after the strike, after the phasing out of the shipyards, he was out of a job. With his farmer's suspicion that the system was rigged against the little fellow, he went back to helping his father on the farm and at the Market.

The atmosphere on Pike Place was more urban than when he worked there before the war. Electric lights framed the sign atop the Leland Hotel. Goodwin had taken over the Rotary Bakery and the doughnut machine had been sped up. Pike Place was paved, and Market-related business—Dunn's Seed Company, Carnation Packing Company, a pork house, a paper bag store, and a Market delivery service—dotted its east side between Pike Street and Virginia.

Hotels and apartments had prospered with the growth of waterfront employment and the construction of the wooden overpass between the wharves and the bluff. The Hotel Livingston, 1931 First Avenue (at the corner of Virginia), boasted "Modern Special Rates by the Week or Month, Grand Sound Views." The LaSalle, 1019 Pike, offered "Modern Steam Heated Rooms," each with hot and cold water, for three dollars a week and up. The Fairmount, at 1907 First Avenue, assured the cautious that its "outside large furnished rooms with bath and phone" not only commanded "a Grand Marine View" but were fireproof. The Silver Oakum Building, which had been erected in 1910, still housed on its ground floor the Gem Egg Market, but

upstairs, upwind of the sour-smelling poultry carcasses, there were cheap apartments much appreciated by seamen and longshoremen.

The greatest difference was in traffic: automobiles far outnumbered carriages; the delivery truck had replaced the delivery cart; Old Dobbin had given way to the Tin Lizzie; pedestrians were less worried about stepping in manure than being bumped by a Maxwell; parking had become a problem.

When the war ended, the tideflat area was solid fill land, laced with roadways as well as railroad tracks, but the First Avenue bluff still posed a problem for

FACING PAGE: *By the 1920s, the Market was part of Seattle's way of life, but the mixture of farmers in city-owned stalls and merchants renting from private owners created political tensions. Asahel Curtis photographed producer and consumer in May 1925. (Washington State Historical Society, photo by Asahel Curtis, 48313)*

ABOVE: *Willard Soames organized the Associated Farmers of Pike Place. (Pike Place Market Preservation and Development Authority, photo by Christine Koons)*

those wishing to reach the business district. Western Avenue, the principal access route to the north end of downtown, was frequently jammed, especially when trucks were unloading at the commission houses. So the Street Department paved Elliott Way, which slants northwestward to the dock from the juncture of Pike Place and Lenora Street. But traffic reaching the top of the bluff via Elliott Way became ensnarled among the farmers' stalls that occupied much of the paving on Pike Place, as did traffic using the traditional route up Western Avenue.

Commercial and industrial interests on the waterfront asked the city to do something to improve traffic flow. The municipal elections after the General Strike had resulted in a city council acutely sensitive to the desires of the business community, especially when couched in terms of Furthering Progress. With little debate, the council passed a resolution decreeing that after September 1, 1920, the farmers' stalls were not to

be permitted in the street at Pike Place, though the private buildings alongside would remain undisturbed.

Repercussions were immediate. The farmers, of course, were indignant. Where were they to go? The unions joined the protest. So did assorted women's groups, whose influence was especially strong since the passage of the national Women's Suffrage Amendment. The women argued not only the benefits of fresh produce and low prices to the

FACING PAGE ABOVE: *Mrs. Belmont Tiffany's visit in September 1920 showcased the Market as a tourist attraction. (*Seattle Times, *September 5, 1920)*

FACING PAGE BELOW: *Old Dobbin was giving way to Henry Ford's Tin Lizzie. View north on Pike Place from Stewart Street, July 19, 1919. (City of Seattle)*

BELOW: *The Livingston at the corner of First and Virginia boasted "Modern Special Rates by Week or Month, Grand Sound Views." (City of Seattle)*

community, but of the amenity, the charm, and beauty of the Public Market on the bluff above the bay.

The case of the pro-Market people was strengthened when Mrs. Belmont Tiffany (of the New York Tiffanys) visited Seattle. A handsome woman who had been decorated with the Croix de Guerre by the French government for her Red Cross work overseas during the First World War, Mrs. Tiffany told reporters that she had heard Seattle's Market compared favorably to Les Halles in Paris. She paid an early morning visit to Pike Place, sweeping through the stall area gowned in black with matching hat and cloak, a single strand of pearls at her throat, a silver fox scarf about her shoulders. Though about to leave town, she found herself unable to resist the temptation of a box of raspberries and, according to the press, when Mrs. Tiffany boarded the ship for Victoria later that morning,

Gotham Leader Goes Marketing

✳ ✳ ✳   ✳ ✳ ✳   ✳ ✳ ✳

Buys Tempting Berries Here

NOTED SOCIETY WOMAN OF NEW YORK

Mrs. Belmont Tiffany.

Although in Seattle only a short time, Mrs. Belmont Tiffany of New York, social leader, horticulturist, author and Red Cross worker, couldn't resist the temptation of a visit to the Public Market here. She emerged with a tempting box of raspberries

Social Leader, Author, Horticulturist and Red Cross Worker Enjoys Brief Excursion Through Public Mart.

she carried "a leather jewel case in one hand and in the other her beloved box of Seattle raspberries."

With the Pike Place stalls getting such favorable publicity, the council relented on its deadline and agreed the farmers could stay on the street until new space for them could be found. The most promising proposals came from private developers.

The Westlake Market Company, which operated a building at Fifth and Virginia in which the city leased stall space for daily rental to farmers, proposed to create a two-floor underground market on Fifth between Stewart and Virginia, which would provide space for 300 stalls, cold and dry storage, wash racks, lockers, and other sanitary facilities. The Westlake people said this market could be operated either under city control or by the Market Company for the use of the farmers as "the officially designated farmers' market."

"EVERYTHING FOR THE
TABLE UNDER ONE ROOF"

A.F. Niemeyer

ARTHUR E. GOODWIN

THIS IS an age of specialization, bringing in its wake greater efficiency and consequent advancement and improvement in our welfare. We find specialists in every walk of life, concentrating their efforts in one particular line of endeavor and rendering a service far more efficient than under the old order of things. ❡ Outstanding in this regard is Arthur E. Goodwin, whose specialty is public markets. For the last seven years Mr. Goodwin has been general manager of the Public Market & Department Store Company, which corporation operates four public markets: The Pike Place Market, the Economy Market, the Outlook Market, and the new Municipal Market building. Besides Mr. Goodwin's activities in Seattle, he is chairman of the advisory board of the Crystal Palace Public Market in San Francisco, one of the largest markets in the country. He is a member of the advisory board of three large public markets in Portland, and one in Bremerton, and is frequently called upon for expert advice in the establishment and operation of markets in other cities. More than fifty eastern cities have drawn upon his knowledge of market operation. ❡ Mr. Goodwin is a nephew of Frank Goodwin, whose vision and genius were responsible for the creation of Seattle's first public market in 1907 and the subsequent establishment of three other markets. Attesting the success attendant somewhat upon Mr. Goodwin's early efforts in the establishment of these markets is the national reputation which Seattle has attained for her superior market system. Seattle holds a position of distinction among American cities in that respect. The huge crowds that daily attend these markets attest the value of the markets to the community. ❡ Seven years ago the reins of management were turned over to Arthur Goodwin, who had understudied the intricacies of market operation for some time previous. He has under his control over 200,000 square feet of rental area, with upwards of 175 tenants. ❡ Born in New York in 1887, he early heard the call of the West and came to Seattle in 1907, entering the real estate business with the Goodwin Real Estate Company, one of the leading realty concerns of the city. He is at present secretary of this organization. Mr. Goodwin is vice-president of the Rotary Bread Stores, a system of chain bakeries, and is secretary-treasurer of the Seattle Inland Oil Company, a local corporation operating in eastern Washington. ❡ Mr. Goodwin is a member of the Seattle Chamber of Commerce, Seattle Yacht Club, the Automobile Club, Japan Society, Young Men's Republican Club, and George Washington Lodge F. & A. M. ❡ In the line of recreation he has made golf his hobby.

The Goodwins proposed an expansion of the off-street facilities near the Pike Place site. Arthur Goodwin had been promoted to general manager of the Public Market & Department Store Company in 1918, but his uncle Frank had the final say on policy and drew the plans for the proposed addition. The Goodwins circulated a letter offering investors seven percent mortgage bonds "to solve the market problems through PRIVATE ENTERPRISE DEPENDING UPON ITS BEING CARRIED OUT WITH THE COOPERATION OF PROPERTY OWNERS AND BUSINESSMEN." The money raised would be used primarily to erect a six-story building on the outboard side of Western Avenue with a connecting sky bridge to the original Market. The Goodwins proposed to lease the city space for up to 300 stalls at a yearly fee of one dollar, provided the city agreed to furnish lights for the public premises, stalls, and sidewalks.

Many farmers expressed reluctance to leave the traditional market area, let alone to being put underground on Fifth Avenue, but the city council leaned toward the Westlake Market Company proposal. They were influenced by Councilman R. H. "That Man" Thomson, former Seattle City Engineer. Thomson had conceived the plans regarding downtown Seattle and saw only progress in any proposal to improve traffic flow. Two of the three members of the council's Harbors and Public Grounds Committee committed themselves to the Westlake proposal, though the chairman, John E. Carroll, remained noncommittal.

The threat of deportation inland led the farmers to begin to organize. Willard Soames and others circulated and signed petitions asking the city to preserve Pike Place as the farmers' market area. The petitioners later formed the Associated

Farmers of the Pike Place Market to represent their interests in dealing with the city and the Market management.

The day of decision came on April 25, 1921. "That Man" Thomson carried the votes of A. T. Drake, William Hickman Moore, and Oliver T. Erickson. Council President R. B. Hesketh was joined by A. L. Cohen, C. B. Fitzgerald, and Philip Tindall in favor of Pike Place. John E. Carroll, chairman of the Harbors and Public Grounds Committee, had the swing vote. He came down on the Pike Place side.

The council followed their selection of site by directing the Public Works Department to work out a lease with the Goodwins for stall space to be occupied by the farmers when they had to vacate the Pike Place pavement. The Goodwins at once began construction of the Municipal Market Building on the sunset side of Western Avenue, the last major addition to the Market area for half a century.

The farmers were still rejoicing in the salvation of their traditional Market site when another famous visitor praised Pike Place. Madame Joseph Jacques Césaire Joffre, wife of the French World War I leader, came to Seattle with her husband in March 1922. The Joffres were guests at the East Highland Drive mansion of Samuel Hill, the railroad tycoon. One morning, Madame Joffre decided to shoo the Hills' cooks out of the kitchen and personally prepare a French dinner for her husband and their hosts. So she went to the Market.

Accompanied by her daughter, Germaine, who carried their shopping basket, she went shopping incognito (though not without an entourage of reporters). Like any thrifty shopper, she made a reconnaissance of the stalls before buying anything, then returned to the places that had caught her fancy. Her first purchase was from a vendor who had promised "Nice lettuce, lady!" When she bought several heads he threw in a bunch of carrots as lagniappe. After filling Germaine's basket to overflow with apples, beets, spinach, radishes, cauliflower, and green onions, she bought a second basket and headed to the meat market in search of sausage: "You see the marshal has his favorite meat."

On another day, Madame Joffre returned with the marshal and their host. A woman running a delicatessen recognized the visitors and, raising a ladle full of green olives from a barrel, offered some to the French woman. Madame Joffre lifted her veil, tasted one, then insisted that the marshal, Sam Hill, and Ulysses S. Grant III share the bounty. A little later, Papa Joffre fell into discussion with a French-speaking farmer on the best way of fertilizing lettuce. He was delighted to learn that the people selling the vegetables actually raised them.

Seattle was charmed by the marshal and his wife, especially by her exclamations about "Such clean food! Such wonderful vegetables!" and her praise of Seattle women: "I like the happy faces of

FACING PAGE AND CENTER: *Frank Goodwin and his nephew, Arthur, dominated the private enterprise sector of the Market. Frank designed and raised money for the original buildings. Arthur became manager of the Public Market & Department Store Company in 1918. (Sketch from* Seattle Leaders; *edited and published by E. M. Desmond, photo courtesy of Mary Bonamy)*

the people, especially the women. Ah, they must all be happy indeed. I have seen many sad faces of women. They were sad in China, and sad in Japan and everywhere it seems the women's faces are sad, except in this glorious city."

A *Seattle Times* editorialist attributed the happiness to "something that lies deep in the roots of American character, American customs and American veneration of womanhood." He added, "One must not forget the markets! Clean, yes, and marvelous of display! They compare favorably with those in other American cities—or foreign cities, for that matter. Mme. Joffre is not the first visitor to be favorably impressed, although she undoubtedly was the first to purchase there the materials for a dinner for a marshal of France."

Another cause for pride was the opening in July 1922 of a branch of the Seattle Public Library at the Market, after workers there had requested the service. The branch, with its thousand books shelved in a former groceteria beside a doughnut shop and above a lard rendering plant in a basement of the Main Market, became the most active in the library system. A *Times* feature writer noted that in spite of "the outdoor noises and smells of the market, the book corner maintains the true library atmosphere of detachment and unruffled serenity."

In its first two months of operation, the branch issued cards to 350 patrons. "The little dry goods clerk of Semitic origin with a penchant for Amy Lowell and gastronomy, the big Scandinavian truck gardener who reads Knut Hamsun in his own language, housewives who want books on garden culture, and gardeners who want books on baby culture, decide the titles on the groceteria shelves.

"The little librarian prides herself

ABOVE: *The Seattle Public Library opened an underground branch library above a lard rendering plant in the basement of the main Market.* (Seattle Times, *March 2, 1924*)

that she seldom loses a patron. Once introduced to the books among the green groceries, the dry goods and the cook shops, finders keep on coming. Some were first lured in by the sight of comfortable chairs looking out over the harbor. Some come in to sit and think, and some just sit. But eventually they take out books."

Unruffled serenity at the Market was limited to the library when the time came in August 1922 for the farmers to move off the pavement and into the new sidewalk stalls in space leased by the city from the Goodwins' Public Market & Department Store Company. The farmers hadn't realized that all the sidewalk space was not reserved for daily renting. The stalls on the sidewalk fronting the south side of Pike Street west of First Avenue were reserved for lease by the company, as were those in the southernmost stretch on the west side of Pike Place. The eight stalls on Pike Street (first known as the Goodwin Group, a designation soon shortened to the GG stalls) lay along the most heavily traveled pedestrian route in the Market.

The farmers felt themselves victims of a swindle. They argued that for the city to turn over this space to a private company for lease to vendors who purchased from middlemen violated the fundamental purpose of a public market. The Goodwins, who felt they had created the Pike Place Market and who had fought off the proposed transfer of the farmers' market to a less scenic site, felt they were victims of ingratitude.

At a meeting attended by 260 grower-vendors at the Labor Temple, the farmers protested against turning over a city sidewalk to a private company to lease for its own profit, protested that renting sidewalk space to non-farmers undercut the purpose of the Market, and protested

the new sliding scale for stall space which set high daily rents for stalls closer to the streetcar stops. Nor were they happy with the way space was assigned.

Arthur Goodwin, speaking for the private company, declared that the city's Market Master had charge of 90 percent of the stall space on the sidewalks; only 10 percent of the sidewalk space under the arcades was reserved for the company. Conceding this was the best commercial space, he argued that it benefited the customers to have it leased to vendors who would be present year-round, not changing haphazardly according to season and the luck of the daily draw.

The controversy caught the attention of Seattle's newly elected mayor, who took office in June 1922. Edwin J. Brown was a specialist at fishing troubled waters. Besides politics, Brown had practiced dentistry, pugilism, palmistry, and unrestrained oratory. He sported a banded straw hat, wore vests that threatened to touch off fire alarms, carried a walking stick, and smiled at everybody, explaining that they often smiled back with teeth he had given them. Doc Brown was in favor of high wages, high employment, low streetcar fares, and leaving the enforcement of Prohibition to the federal government. He was against drunk drivers, corporate sin, earwigs, and days in which his name failed to appear in the headlines.

The Mayor assigned the city superintendent of buildings to make a study of the Market situation, but before the report was drafted he announced that it would show that the City of Seattle, through its health department, was linked hand-in-hand with the Food Trust. Brown complained that it took him fifteen minutes to make his way from the armory to the Oriental bazaar that was the Market. He offered an offhand solution: the city should buy up a city block or two away from the bluff and build a more convenient emporium. It would only cost two or three million dollars.

"The time has come to an end when we should compel the people to go along a narrow cowpath and buy their supplies at one man's property," the Mayor told a reporter for the *Union Record*. "Let's buy a block, two blocks if necessary, up there in the district back and beyond the New Washington Hotel on Olive Street and put in a modern market that can be reached by all the people from four sides. Put a wide thoroughfare through the middle. Make it readily accessible on four streets."

Brown's suggestion alarmed parties on both sides of the controversy. The farmers didn't really want to move from Pike Place. They loved Pike Place. What they wanted was access to the best space, and lower stall fees. And the Goodwins didn't want the city putting up a building to compete with the privately owned market buildings around Pike Place.

Arthur Goodwin ran newspaper advertisements inviting the public to "Come and see the winding cowpaths of this Oriental Bazaar! They are wide enough now for the great cow that jumped over the moon." The farmers threatened a strike. If the stall arrangements were not changed, they'd set up tents at Fourth and Stewart and sell vegetables from there. But the disputants got together and papered over their differences, which may have been what Doc Brown had anticipated. He was not without political shrewdness.

The farmers were given access to stalls closer to Pike Street, though the company retained control of the eight GG stalls. Market Master John Winship came up with a more acceptable system of distributing the stalls. They divided the Market into a flower section, a meat section, a dry row, and a wet row, each with its own rotation system, so that every farmer had a turn in the more favorably located stalls. Fees varied from ten cents for stalls at the northern end of the Market—Siberia—to twenty-five and fifty cents for those on the more frequented aisles in the Sunny South. If a vendor in a high-priced stall sold out his produce and went home before closing time, another vendor could move south by paying the difference between the fee for his original stall and the vacated one. Farmers still resented the company's control of the GG stalls, but their truce held for several years.

Doc Brown, meanwhile, kept talking about the possibility of a new market. He revived memories of his remark about the "bazaar at the end of a cowpath" with a bizarre publicity stunt. He arranged to have a trained Holstein bull that was appearing in a vaudeville show brought to the Mayor's office in the Municipal Building. Reporters might mumble that there was enough bull around the place already, but photographers thought it would provide good pictures. They liked the idea even better when a woman revivalist entered the office with a basket of Bibles and an American flag. When she saw the bull she climbed onto a table, held out a Bible and cried, "Kneel to God!" Kneeling was a command the bull knew. It went down on its front knees in obeisance.

During the 1924 municipal election campaign, Doc Brown amplified his original proposal. He unveiled a sketch by architect John Graham, Sr., who had just designed the Dexter Horton Building. It showed a mammoth concrete structure ten stories high, three blocks long, stretching north from First and Pike, extending westward over Pike Place, over Western Avenue, over Railroad Avenue, and front-

ing on the waterfront near the municipal ferry dock.

Brown's fantasy in concrete was to include a cold storage plant, space for hundreds of farmers, a civic auditorium seating thousands, a floor with space available for "infant industries," and facilities for a municipal radio station which then would have been in the infant industry class. The Mayor said the city building superintendent thought the edifice could be built for $800,000 but "Why be cheap? Why not spend two million and get a real market, with a roof garden and observatory?"

Money wouldn't be a problem anyway, the Mayor went on, because the Market wouldn't cost the taxpayer anything. He'd issue bonds to pay for construction and pay them off out of rental. Seattle would build on a pay-as-you-grow basis: the first unit would be only 125 feet wide, one story high at First Avenue, but about ten stories seen from the tideflats. "When we get half a million people we'll build another unit, two blocks south.

Then when we get a million population we'll build a third unit two blocks north."

As for the roof garden and observatory, how else could Seattle reveal its wonders to visitors? "You have to send 'em out on a patrol boat now to look at the waterfront," Doc said. "Another thing: we'd own the Market, instead of the present public market owning us."

Doc Brown kept talking about his dream market as long as he was in office. He used the John Graham sketch in his campaign literature in 1926 but neither the Mayor nor his community palace survived the election.

Frank Goodwin was sixty years old and tired of the politics and personalities involved in running the Public Market & Department Store Company. He wanted

ABOVE: *Mayor Edwin J. Brown (center), shown here with Vice President Calvin Coolidge (left), tried to solve the conflict by proposing a new public market farther inland.* (Seattle Post-Intelligencer)

more time for his inventions and his investments. Shortly before Christmas 1925, he remarked to his nephew Arthur that he'd like to sell the Market.

How much are you asking?

It would take half a million cash. That's for the business. I'd keep the real property.

That night Arthur told his wife Caroline that it was his opportunity of a lifetime. The company dominated an area that drew 25,000 shoppers a day Monday through Friday, and twice as many on Saturdays when 600 farmers competed for 500 stalls. The twelve markets around Pike Place were grossing an estimated $30,000,000 business for the year. He knew the business, he was called for consultations all over the country, he had published a book on the subject, and he had nearly a decade of experience as a manager. What he didn't have was half a million dollars.

Arthur talked to friends and associates. Walter Taylor, a boyhood chum from New York who had come west on his advice and was co-owner with him of the Rotary Bakery, agreed to invest. The Manning brothers, whose Pike Place Coffee House Restaurant had spawned a coast-wide chain of coffee houses, put up some money. So did Joe Desimone, an Italian farmer and vendor who had been one of the first to rent a GG stall. But more would be needed.

On an afternoon late in December, Caroline Goodwin drove her husband to a two o'clock appointment at the National Bank of Commerce. She found parking for the Packard, wrapped herself in the car robe, and settled down for a long wait while Arthur argued with the bankers. He returned in a few minutes from what had been a brief interview. The bankers had objected that the Market was little more than a group of glorified apple boxes, a poor risk. Arthur had replied that was what made it such an attractive investment; it was a great moneymaker if properly maintained. They said that, on second thought, he was correct and agreed to loan him $375,000, floating that amount in First Mortgage and Leasehold Gold Bonds, guaranteed on principal and interest by Goodwin himself.

Final details of the purchase were worked out at a conference between Arthur and his uncles at Frank Goodwin's house on Lake Washington. A new company, Pike Place Public Markets, Inc., was formed with a capitalization announced as "above $700,000." Arthur became president and general manager; Walter Taylor, vice president; C. W. Stier, secretary and treasurer, and Frank Clifford, who had been rental manager under Frank, moved up to assistant manager. Pike Place Public Markets received a fee simple title to the Pike Place Market building and leases on the Economy Market and Municipal Market buildings. Frank Goodwin, through a corporation named the Pike Investment Company, retained title to the sloping hillside west of Pike Place.

Even before the transfer became official on January 1, 1926, Arthur hired a contractor to build a new office, big as a banker's and glowing with mahogany, on the second floor of the Economy Market. He greatly admired his uncle ("Credit is due Frank Goodwin for whatever has been accomplished in lowering the cost of living in this city through the medium of public markets"), but if one thing was

---

FACING PAGE: *Doc Brown's idea of moving the Market to Olive Street was replaced by turning the First Avenue cliff into a high-rise combination of vegetable stands, industrial areas, civic auditorium, and radio station. Architect John Graham, Sr., sketched this vision of the future. (City of Seattle)*

going to change at Pike Place during his administration, it was style. No more desks in the bowels of the building next to the public lavatory.

The Pike Place Public Market offices were ten times as large as the Public Market & Department Store Company's old hideaway. There were drapes, carpets, bookshelves and books, a huge conference table, a tiled fireplace. Company stationery blossomed with an engraving of the Market buildings, the Sound, the Olympics, and the company name against a background of sky and water.

Arthur's personal style was clearly different from his uncle's. Frank had been a member of the respected clubs—his favorite was the Arctic—but his idea of a good time was reading *The Wall Street Journal.* Arthur liked to entertain. He moved into a colonial-style house, Goodwin Manor, with four ivory columns at the front entrance, a formal dining room seating thirty, a breakfast room, ballroom, music room, and billiard room. There was also a rose garden, a badminton court, and in the garage, a turntable for the family Packard.

In this setting he entertained city council members, visiting governors, the Shah of Persia, and especially theater people. He had grown up around actors and was incurably stagestruck. He also became a founder of the Seattle Repertory Theatre in the University District.

Arthur's love of the theater was reflected in changes he made at the Market. He recognized the dramatic value of the setting and had the lighting improved, instituted a program of continual painting of the stalls, and extended flower boxes over the marquee from First Avenue to Pike Place. He persuaded the merchants to group their advertising in a full-page spread on Thursday afternoons, and staged weekend events to boost crowds. When patronage at the stalls in the new Municipal Market Building across Western Avenue proved disappointing, he hired vaudeville performers to put on daily shows. The Crystal Market in Tacoma took up the idea and there was talk of a Fruit Stand Circuit.

Arthur's innovations got a favorable review in *Variety.* The voice of show biz said that with "vaude as a puller, the public markets are doing a land office biz. Market vaude is done in presentation style with an M. C. announcing the turns. Five shows daily are offered, with change day being Saturday. Customers are given folding chairs and they act as their own ushers. The floor of the markets can take care of over 1,500 with no overhead outside of the small salaries involved. The acts are paid off partly in oranges, apples, etc. The balance consists of salaries running from a starting $2.50 to a stellar turn drawing $5."

Marketing techniques might be changing, but an aspect of Pike Place that proved impervious to the passage of time was controversy about the GG stalls. In April 1926, the militant farmers put on a show of their own.

The Harbors and Public Grounds Committee of the city council was holding a routine business meeting. Principal on the agenda was the Pike Place Public Market Company request for a fifteen-year extension of the city's lease of sidewalk space at the old Public Market & Department Store Company. The three committeemen and staff members were in their seats, and representatives of the new Pike Place Market Company were preparing to make a short presentation, when a crowd of nearly two hundred farm men and women, most of them in work clothes, some carrying hand-painted signs, others carrying children, swarmed into the chamber.

They identified themselves as the Associated Farmers of the Pike Place Market. Their spokesman, a lean man with brown hair, brown eyes, a strong nose, and thin lips, identified himself as Willard Soames—the same Soames who had sold chickens with his father on the dry row, worked in shipyards during the war, and signed a petition supporting the Goodwins during the period when moving the Market was proposed, but who still felt betrayed by the city's lease of sidewalks to a corporation that subleased to vendors who didn't raise the crops they sold. The Market had been created to eliminate the middleman. Pushing the farmers into stalls farther north, Soames told the council in a notably messed-up simile, "was just like taking bread and butter out of the farmer's pocket. When you put them out there, well, you might as well put them out in the country and leave them there."

Soames knew there was nothing fresh in this argument; the farmers had tried it time after time without getting the GG space for growers. The trouble, he decided, was not with the argument but with the council; the farmers needed the help of someone who knew how to fight city hall. Labor leaders he asked for advice directed him to the Collins Building at Second and James where the Legal Defense Department of the Seattle Central Labor Council had a small office. There he found a champion in George Vanderveer.

Soames knew of Vanderveer, of course. He'd been raising hell in and around Seattle for years. Everybody in Seattle knew of Vanderveer and most held strong opinions about him. The establishment regarded him as a drunk, a

ABOVE: *Under Arthur Goodwin's administration, the Public Market & Department Store Company stepped up its advertising campaigns, installed flower boxes on the Pike Street marquee, improved the lighting, and even staged free vaudeville shows in the Municipal Market Building. (Seattle Star, November 27, 1928)*

womanizer, and—worse—a dangerously effective defender of impermissible thoughts and deeds. Others regarded him as a friend of the workingman, a fighter for free speech, a defender (often for free) of social outcasts. A graduate of Stanford and the Columbia Law School, Vanderveer once defined for the benefit of a court his relationship to the downtrodden: "I speak with feeling because I am one of them . . . because there is something undeniable within me that compels me without mercy to my inescapable destiny . . . to serve as Counsel for the Damned."

The counsel was a wiry man with close-cropped, thinning hair. He affected steel-rimmed spectacles and was in shirtsleeves when Soames met him. He had the quick, compact moves of a welterweight and jabbed the air with a lean forefinger when asking questions. He rolled cigarettes one-handed from a Bull Durham bag and punctuated Soames's answers about the farmers' grievances with cynical remarks concerning their chances of getting fair treatment from officials. Soames thought him "one of the greatest lawyers that ever lived," and was delighted when Vanderveer agreed to represent the Associated Farmers.

Vanderveer fought for the farmers—or, more precisely, against the Goodwins—not only before the council but in the courts and in the press. No one was more skilled than the Counsel for the Damned in trying a case before the bar of public opinion. Like Arthur Goodwin, he had a taste for show biz.

The idea of the first demonstration in the council chambers was certainly his. He stage-managed subsequent hearings before the Harbors and Public Grounds Committee and the full council so that the public would perceive them as contests pitting simple men in overalls,

horny-handed sons of toil with the mud of the land they tilled clinging to their boots, against double-breasted lawyers lusting after technicalities and businessmen beet red at threats to undeserved profits.

The initial confrontation between Soames and the council committee led to the presentation of a petition asking for a formal hearing on their grievances, Written by Vanderveer on Legal Defense Department stationery that bore the motto "One for All and All for One," it concluded:

> To summarize, I am advised that the successor to the Public Market and Dept. Store Company occupies and leases 120 front feet of stall space in Pike Place. That is divided into stalls with a frontage of five feet each which, I am advised, rent at $75 per month. In other words, the total revenue is approximately $1800.
>
> These stalls are all on public property. They were constructed pursuant to the ordinance and contract above mentioned. None of them, with a single exception [Joe Desimone], are leased to producers. All of them, with the same exception, are leased to competitors of the producers. The rental is, of course, absorbed and paid by the purchaser who believes he is getting home-grown produce but isn't. The same company received a revenue of approximately $750 a month from other stalls likewise constructed on public property on the bridges across Western Avenue . . .
>
> The rent charged by this company to the tenants in its own Pike Place Market Building is perhaps the highest paid for any similar market space in this city, and such space is

considered the most desirable of any market space in this city for the principal reason that it is regarded by the public as a place where they may buy fresh locally grown produce directly from the producer. All this is a direct fraud upon the consumer and a direct outrage upon the rights of the producer.

Manifestly, if the conditions at this market are as I have described them they should be remedied, and I respectfully request that your body call a special meeting at which evidence may be heard of the truth of all these matters, and at which you may learn in the most direct and authoritative manner how your public streets are being misused and the purpose of your ordinance perverted.

Arthur Goodwin, with advice from his attorney, W. D. Lane, replied on a Pike Place Market letterhead that, some noted, showed buildings but no farmers. After reviewing the history of the contract and the improvements the Public Market & Department Store Company had built and paid for, he took up the question of revenue:

Mr. Vanderveer next goes into the matter of the revenues that the market company derives from the "GG" spaces. The revenues which are derived from this, and also from the space on the bridge reserved by the market company, constitute the compensation to which the market company is entitled because of the investment they have in these improvements. He states that none of these stalls are leased to producers. Nothing in our city contract specifies that they are either to be leased to

producers or nonproducers. He states that the rent is, of course, absorbed and paid by the purchaser. That is true in all business.

We do not see how either Mr. Vanderveer or his farmers are concerned with the revenues we derive from our properties and the space which we hold under contract with the city.

ABOVE: *George F. Vanderveer served as attorney for the Associated Farmers of the Pike Place Market. He once said, "I speak with feeling . . . because there is something undeniable within me that compels me without mercy to my inescapable destiny . . . to serve as Counsel for the Damned." (Mary Randlett Collection)*

ARTHUR E. GOODWIN, PRESIDENT AND GEN'L MANAGER
JOE DESIMONE, VICE PRESIDENT
JOHN CLIFFORD, SECRETARY
C. W. STIER, TREASURER

GENERAL OFFICES
ROOMS 6-7-8
ECONOMY PUBLIC MARKET
1431 FIRST AVENUE

PIKE PLACE
PUBLIC MARKETS
INCORPORATED

OPERATING —
PIKE PLACE PUBLIC MARKET
ECONOMY PUBLIC MARKET
OUTLOOK PUBLIC MARKET
MUNICIPAL MARKET BUILDING

SEATTLE, WASH.
November 2, 1927

The fact remains that no other market company in this district has provided spaces for farmers or sidewalks in order to create space for farmers; or built any buildings for the use of farmers; or designed, planned and stimulated additions and extensions to the city's market; nor do we see any move on the part of Mr. Vanderveer or his farmers to raise funds to provide additional space or to improve the present market; or any constructive idea advanced for the improvement of the market as a whole. He covets the space which we rightfully acquired five years ago and offers nothing for it. It would be just as ridiculous for him to demand space at the Bon Marche at the Corner of Second and Pike. His whole petition is based on the destruction of property and the whole city agreement was based on the construction of property.

These missives were directed to the Harbors and Public Grounds Committee, chaired by Oliver T. Erickson. The Seattle Municipal League, which regarded the antediluvian Roland Hartley as a "sound governor," described Erickson as "unfriendly to large financial interests and generally considered an ultra radical." Sixty-eight years old, born before the Civil War, a carpenter by trade, a union man for more than forty years, Erickson's philosophy was rooted in the ideas of the Populist era. Even after fifteen years on the city council he believed in municipal ownership of utilities, including sidewalks. He set May 4 as the date for a hearing by his committee on the questions raised by Vanderveer.

The hearing was held in a chamber packed with members of Associated Farmers. Testimony followed the pattern of the written statements already on the record. The first dramatic moment came when Arthur Goodwin, responding to a question as to what the result would be if the company lost control of the GG stalls, responded that it would "bankrupt us," then reminded the councilmen, "We made the Market." The audience responded with an unruly chorus of "No! No!" and "The Farmers made it!"

ABOVE: *During the controversy over control of space in the Market, the Associated Farmers liked to point out that the Pike Place Public Market letterhead showed a marvelous vista, an array of buildings, but no farmers. (University of Washington Libraries, Special Collections, J. D. Ross Papers)*

Vanderveer scored a telling point when Corporation Counsel Thomas Kennedy described the arrangement under which the Public Market & Department Store Company had been given control of the GG space as a gentleman's agreement. He conceded that, in his opinion, the city could not legally turn over a street or sidewalk to a private company.

Goodwin at this point suggested a compromise: his company would extend the Pike Place Arcade as far as Virginia, creating additional stalls which would be allocated by the city-appointed Market Master. Farmers protested that would shove them still farther north. Vanderveer said, "All we want is a chance for the producing farmers of this community to have stalls where they can sell the stuff they produce, direct to the consumer." Chairman Erickson recessed the meeting to give the committee time, as he put it, "to arrange some new program which would enable the city to get back its street."

With the company on the defensive, Goodwin wrote a personal letter to Erickson. Pointing out that the new Pike Place Public Market Company had been created in the belief that existing arrangements with the city would be continued and that company bonds had been "more or less widely circulated," he said that "it is to our mutual interest, myself as an organizer of the company and yourself as an official of the City, to try to get together and protect this investment . . . I am writing you thus personally to ask if it would not be possible to sit down in privacy and try to work out a satisfactory working agreement." Erickson felt such a meeting would be inappropriate.

The first hearing had been a public relations triumph for Vanderveer, calling attention to the farmers' complaints and raising serious doubts about the company's arrangement with the city. During subsequent hearings, however, splits were revealed in the farmers' ranks. Racial motivations became apparent.

Some of the antagonism against the Goodwins, it developed, stemmed from the belief of some Caucasian farmers that the GG stalls served as outlets for produce sold to middlemen by commission houses owned by Japanese. Washington State's alien land law, which was aimed at Asians, was being used to prevent the Japanese not only from owning land but also from renting it. Some of the Associated Farmers claimed that the Goodwins and Market Master Grant Stevens were engaged in an elaborate conspiracy to allocate stalls in such a way that white farmers could not sell their goods directly to customers and so had to sell to Japanese wholesalers who then sold to middlemen, mixing in produce grown illegally by Japanese aliens.

As the testimony became more complex and abrasive, the members of the Harbors and Public Grounds Committee interpreted the problem differently. For Erickson, the question was how to get the sidewalk back under city control. For Councilman E. L. Blaine, the question was whether it would be right to abrogate a contract that both parties had entered in good faith. For Councilman Philip Tindall, the question was what would be in the best interest of the patrons of the Market.

Not until October 1927 did the issue come to a vote in the city council. Erickson proposed an amendment to the Market ordinance that would bar the company from selling fruit and produce in its stalls. His motion lost on a tie vote, four to four. The council then referred to Corporation Counsel Kennedy the question of whether the company was barred under its contract with the city from leasing the GG stalls to firms in competition with farmers selling their own produce. Nothing had been resolved.

Vanderveer and the Associated Farmers now attacked on two new fronts. They filed formal complaints with the city council's Department Efficiency Committee charging the city's Market Master with corruption and favoritism, and they went to court seeking a writ of mandamus that would force the Pike Place Market Company to remove its stalls from a city sidewalk.

Grant Stevens had succeeded John Winship as Market Master in 1923. His qualifications for the post were that he had a degree in business administration from the University of Washington, that his father was City Sanitary Engineer, and that he would work for $170 a month. His liabilities, at least according to the press, were that this was his first job, he made enemies easily, and his wife had expensive tastes. The specific charge against him was that he had suspended from access to stalls a Japanese man, M. Shikata, who had sold rhubarb neither he nor his employer had cultivated, but upon receipt of a "loan" of twenty dollars had allowed Mr. Shikata to resume his business in the Market.

Otto A. Case, a veteran politician with an eye ever on higher office, chaired the council committee hearing the charges. There wasn't much doubt about the hot rhubarb case. Shikata swore he had given the money, Stevens admitted taking it and resigned "to clear the air." But Case then expanded the investigation from the particulars about Stevens to the general efficiency of Market administration. Everybody was interested since nearly everybody shopped at the Market sometime during the year. Chairman Case provided the press with the sort of scandal city editors most love: colorful characters

with more notoriety than clout admitting to practices not universally acknowledged.

Before long, Joe Desimone was on the stand jovially testifying that, sure, he gave baskets of cabbage to market inspectors. Of course. Why not? He gave them to the city councilmen too if they came by, and he sent baskets of flowers to their houses. Small stuff indeed, but Desimone was not only the sole holder of a GG stall who was also a bona fide producer, but had bought out Walter Taylor's interest in the Pike Place Public Market Company in 1927 and was now its vice president.

The papers were in rare agreement even as to simile. The Market Administration smelled like rotten cabbage. The Prosecuting Attorney started an investigation but found nothing to prosecute. A new Market Master was appointed. The city council studied the Market and reported that under previous administrations, practices had been lax. The story died out.

The Associated Farmers of Pike Place Market's fight against the Pike Place Public Market Company climaxed with the trial in Judge Robert Jones's court on the question of whether the GG stalls were a public nuisance.

J. W. Vandervort, a member of the Associated Farmers who raised crops in the White River valley, was the petitioner. He objected to the blocking of the sidewalks by the stalls in front of the Pike Place Market Building and asked the court to direct the Board of Public Works to have them removed. Vanderveer represented Vandervort; Corporation Counsel Kennedy represented the Board of Public Works; no less than four legal firms had representatives on hand to look after the Goodwin interests. Frank Goodwin, the man most responsible for the physical layout of the Market, was present as a witness, as was Arthur. The spectators'

area was packed with farm folk of assorted races and opinions.

Frank Goodwin testified at length about the arrangements that had led to the creation of the stalls on the sidewalk. The object had been not greed but to meet a need, to get the farmers off the Pike Place street so traffic could flow. But for the stalls now to be removed, he said, "would destroy two-thirds of the investment of the whole market property. It would be a losing proposition."

Under cross-examination Vanderveer asked, "Would you not concede the company would not lose anything as a matter of law? It does not own what is on the city street. It can't lose what it does not own."

Arthur Goodwin's testimony revealed that the company was realizing $5,000 a week in rentals. Vanderveer was delighted to get that on the record. "We admit that to remove the stalls will work a hardship on Goodwin's public market company," he told the court in summary. "Any company which is making such unholy profits will naturally be inconvenienced to have that revenue cut off."

Goodwin's attorney, W. D. Lane, went after Vandervort as a stalking horse for Soames and the Associated Farmers.

ABOVE: *Some of the antagonism against the Goodwins stemmed from the belief of some Caucasian farmers that GG stalls served as outlets for produce sold to middlemen by commission houses owned by Japanese. (Washington State Historical Society, photo by Asahel Curtis, November 3, 1926, 50876)*

When Vandervort testified that his occupation was "raising small berries, fruits and vegetables to sell at the public market, Lane pointed out that his farm was miles away from Pike Place. His interest was not that of a citizen wanting to walk beside the street but in damaging the Goodwins, Lane contended.

Vanderveer objected that it didn't matter where Vandervort lived, that "I can have fifty people, I can have five thousand people intervene in here. I have only to yell to the Labor Temple to get as many as I want. . . . If the man is a taxpayer, if he is a resident, as they concede he is, then I don't care whether he is a bootlegger, moonshiner, whether he has been in the penitentiary or what he may do on the side, he has decided on the exercise if that right which the Supreme Court says he has to bring suit. If they are not satisfied with the party we have here I will have a thousand here; we will make a real issue of this thing, a political issue as well as a legal issue, if anybody wants to."

After closing arguments, Judge Jones toured the Market with two guides, Frank Goodwin and George Vanderveer. The conversation must have been remarkable.

Judge Jones waited five months before rendering a decision. During that period Vanderveer told reporters that the farmers realized the judge might rule that all the sidewalk stalls, not just those belonging to the company, would have to be removed from the sidewalk. If so, the farmers would demand that the city provide alternative space. If the city refused, the farmers would establish a farmer-owned cooperative public market center for producers exclusively.

If this was a bluff, the bluff was called. On November 30, 1928, Judge Jones ruled that neither the company nor the city had a right to block the sidewalk with stalls. He gave them four months to clear the walkway of obstructions.

Seattle again found itself faced with the relocation of the farmers' market. Almost no one wanted that. Farmers, housewives, businessmen, union leaders, community club spokesmen, all demanded something be done. The Goodwins and the city appealed Judge Jones' ruling to the State Supreme Court.

Women's organizations deluged the council with demands that the Market somehow be saved. "I have seen the Market grow from a huckster's stand of three wagons," declared Mrs. A. E. Schutt of the Alki Community Club. "I remem-

ber the first day the wagons were there. I believe everyone in Alki who had been downtown that day came home laden with all the vegetables she could carry for twenty-five cents."

"It would be worse than a pity if we should lose the Market," said Mrs. W. H. Utter of the Women's City Club. "We certainly shall not stand idly by."

The legislature met in January. King County legislators introduced a bill which would permit cities to use streets or sidewalks for public markets. It passed. Governor Hartley, sensing socialism, vetoed it.

The city council rushed through an ordinance vacating the portions of Pike Place on which the stalls stood and Mayor Frank Edwards signed it. The Pike Place Market Company built more stalls at the north end of the Market, turned them over to the city for $14,000, and the city granted the company use of the GG stall area.

On March 20, 1930, the State Supreme Court overturned Judge Jones's decision ordering that the sidewalks be cleared. They based their decision on the argument that Vandervort lived too far from the Market to be inconvenienced by the stalls and hence had no standing in court.

By then the country was in the grip of the Great Depression. There were more important things to worry about.

FACING PAGE: *Repercussions from the uproar over the Market were felt over a wide area. The Bryn Mawr Greenhouse on Lake Washington, for instance, was one of the suppliers of seedlings to the embattled farmers. (Washington State Historical Society, photo by Asahel Curtis, 20054)*

Chapter 5 | THE GREAT DAYS OF THE DEPRESSION

Astrange exuberance suffuses the recollections of many old-timers when they talk about depression days at the Market. They acknowledge suffering and misery, but what wells up in memory is the sense of community, the blurring of distinctions between races and nationalities, between seller and customer. "It was like a village in the old country," a Slovene fisherman says. "Everybody felt like he knew everybody."

The frills were gone. The public library closed its Market branch. Arthur Goodwin's Fruit & Vegetable vaudeville troupe withered on the vine. Continuous painting had been discontinued, and foragers took care of much of the garbage removal. Old men played cribbage in vacant stalls, while hobos with gunnysacks tied round their shoes warmed themselves by packing-box bonfires.

Under a sign that warned "NO LOITERING: By order of the Police Department," soapbox speakers expounded on Technocracy, the Townsend Plan, the Commonwealth Federation, and other shortcuts to utopia. The "Spit 'n Argue" gang debated the issues of the world: Who or what was better, Lincoln or Washington, Schmeling or Sharkey, New Deal or Fascism? A reporter for the *Star* spent an afternoon listening in.

I'll take Lincoln alongside of Washington any day. Washington was a great man, all right, but I don't believe he was as great as Lincoln. It wasn't as hard for Washington to get where he got as it was for Lincoln. Now, say, if Lincoln and Washington were here today . . .

The short, stocky man with a black mustache aroused only mild interest in his comparison. People around him, leaning against the railing under the roof, carried on their own conversations as he spoke. Those closest to him—one in overalls, another in mackinaw and the stagged pants of a logger—listened impatiently, waiting their turns.

Three interpretations of the Bible followed: One speaker sought to save the world through Bible readings in the public schools. Another disputed Jesus' ability to walk on water. The third was concerned with the alcoholic content of the water that became wine. Debate was more general about boxing. Had Jack Sharkey deliberately fouled Max Schmeling because the tide of the fight was turning? Would Jack Dempsey fight again? Somebody remembered seeing Dempsey fight out at White Center during his hobo days, and somebody else knew it wasn't Dempsey.

Discussion followed on the corruption of a state legislator, women's attire, the Supreme Court, the effect of repeal of Prohibition on the price of beer, the way to get an able-bodied seaman's ticket, and the evil of women's smoking. Darkness closed in and the men shuffled off in search of warmth.

It wasn't all lounging and loafing. There were the interlocking searches for bargains, customers, and jobs. Farm

Facing page: *During the depression, Rathskeller's Tavern was the workingman's club. Initiative 80, available for signing on the counter, called for relaxation of liquor regulations. It never came to a vote. (City of Seattle)*

Below: *Laurie Olin roamed the Market and Pioneer Square, sketching the walking wounded of the great collapse. (Sketch from* Breath on the Mirror)

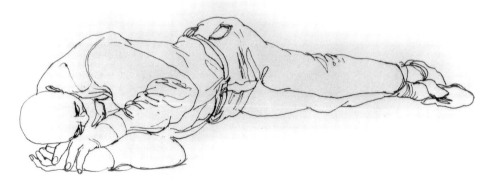

folk needing cash to pay bills and taxes overflowed the covered stalls and spilled again into the street. People like Mr. and Mrs. Emil Schmid, who lived on the east side of Lake Washington, rose around 3 A.M., milked cows, fed chickens, loaded their old flivver with fryers and eggs, drove to Medina, took the ferry across Lake Washington, and reached the Market about six to await stall allotment. On good days they were under cover in the dry row, on bad days out in the rain. When you were out in the rain you had to give bargains to lure customers. The Schmids had to scramble for chicken feed.

Their customers might be even worse off. Mildred Masterson, a sob-sister columnist for the *Seattle Star*, wrote about a woman, down to her last two bits, who went to the Market to ward off starvation:

She found a place where she could get a loaf of bread for a nickel or two for six cents. She got two loaves. She bought a nickel's worth of cheese. She didn't know you could get so much cheese for a nickel, and it's rich, too. She bought a dime's worth of potatoes, and picked them out carefully. She had four cents left.

She lived for four days on the food. On the fourth day she found work. . . . She has a job now, and a comfortable room, warm clothing and three meals a day. But she never spends a quarter without a funny, quivery feeling . . .

Younger women needing work could freelance at the dime-a-dance ballrooms. Another *Star* feature writer reported on a night she spent as a hostess in the Arcadia at First and Pike:

I worked myself and worked the guests from 8:30 till 12:30. Nobody knew I was not "regular." Hostesses

are the only girls in the halls. It is their job to see to the entertainment of the men present. A girl asks a man to dance. He pays her 10 cents for every minute and one-half he dances. She gets five cents and the management gets five. If she inveigles him into buying refreshments she gets a commission.

I passed through the hands of Mama Gilliam, the matron, who took my name, address, parents' residence and name of the last school I attended. I was introduced to the "girls" as "Terry Ferris, the new one."

Eenie, meenie, minie, mo. I chose my first partner like that. He was a tall, handsome stevedore. He asked me if I had an engagement after the dance. I said yes. He asked me if I had an engagement after the engagement. I said yes. And would I go to Portland with him Wednesday? No. All right—he guessed he'd leave. No iniquity there that can't be found in smarter circles.

Then there was the chemist— well-educated and inquisitive. He

---

FACING PAGE: *Men with their bottle in a bag in Laurie Olin's sketch.*

ABOVE: *There was taxi dancing in the Economy Market Building, and traffic went one way the other way on Pike Street during the depression, but the Market of more than half a century ago is immediately recognizable in this* Seattle Times *photo.*

danced 11 dances and tipped well. He supplied coffee and sandwiches. Asked a lot of questions and disappeared. And there was the garbage man, who couldn't be cheated on the number of dances he'd had. He counted the tickets.

Quitting time and still no iniquity. Well, there should be an angle in the exit. Surely there would be pickups. There wasn't. The girls left by the Pike Street entrance, the men by the main door. A pretty blonde helped me find my way out, after I'd turned my badge in and promised to be back Thursday night.

ABOVE: *Theresa De Martini, "the lady of the wheelbarrow," was a familiar figure in the Market of the thirties.* (Seattle Times)

FACING PAGE:*When David Mossafer came to the Market in 1912, everybody called him Dave. Later it was "Papa," and still later "Grandpa." Here, in 1963, he checks the grapes with his son, Joseph.* (Seattle Times)

In the foreground, transients; in the background, the storekeepers, the regulars who had a specialty and had found space in the Market. They clung to their places against the force of economic tides, accreting like coral until they were part of the structure of the place.

Dan Zido was in his teens when he arrived in Seattle in 1906, an apprentice sausage maker from Poland. He dreamed of running a meat market of his own. It took ten years before he earned enough stuffing sausage at the Frye Packing Plant to be able to open a butcher shop in partnership with a man named Ziegler. In 1924, Zido bought out Ziegler and moved into a shop at the south end of the Pike Place Market Building.

Dan's Meats gained the patronage of the local Polish community, then of Greeks, which was important. In the 1920s, Greeks ran most of the larger restaurants in town, including the Orpheum, the Apollo, the Athens, and the Golden Gate. They appreciated the steady quality of Dan's meats, the willingness with which he gave special service, and his acceptance of the fact that sometimes restaurants might be slow to pay. Dan and his patrons sustained each other through the depression. With recovery, he was in position to become wholesaler to most of the city's quality restaurants.

David Mossafer started working in the Market on April 6, 1912, and retired at the age of eighty-three on October 15, 1971. Over the years he was known to an extraordinary range of people in his adopted town. They called him Dave, then Papa, finally Grandpa. No man in the Market was more popular.

In 1912, Mossafer and his brother-in-law Marco Franco opened the Quality Fruit Shop at the corner of Pike Street and Pike Place. Mornings they bought fruit from the commission houses along Western Avenue. The wholesalers—among them A. B. Garrett, Ralph Reed, J. B. Powles, Batford & Company, and Acme Fruit—advised them about the taste, popularity, and storage quality of the various varieties. (Through time, the partners watched sadly as the varieties of apples available to them slowly diminished from thirty to seven under the impact of mass orcharding.) In the early days, the brothers-in-law hired a beer wagon to bring the boxes of fruit up the hill at two cents a box. Some years there were half a million boxes. As the business developed, Marco became the buyer, and David ran the stand, meeting everybody.

"There were only a few papa-mama stores," he said in explanation of his fame and popularity, "so everyone came to the market. I treated everybody equal.

I'm a very democratic fellow. You see, I believe in religion where the God says, 'Everybody is equal and everybody is important to himself.' If you've got a million dollars and the other guy five cents, to me it makes no difference. Today you got the million dollars—tomorrow you might not have any.

"One day a while ago, it was summertime, a fellow comes along, you know, fellow working on the highway, cement all over him. He used to come every week and I was waiting on him. A lady comes up, nice dressed and says, 'Can you wait on me right away?' I said, 'I'm sorry, lady, the gentleman is first.' She got mad.

"About a half-hour later she came back and apologized for acting that way. I says, 'Girl, you born in this country? You know, we are very tolerant people, very democratic. You see this man over there with those dirty overalls? I can take this man and give him good shower and good suit and you would think he was president of the bank. I don't live that way, not on the way he dresses. His money is just as good as yours.' She said, 'I'm sorry. You give me a good lesson.' That lady, she became my good customer and good friend."

In 1928, Mossafer and Ness Peha started United Fruit Company, the first locally owned chain of supermarkets in the Seattle area. There were two stores on First Avenue and others at 85th and Greenwood, in the University District, at West Seattle junction, and in Bremerton. They had one good year; then came the crash and the depression. Wholesalers couldn't give credit, and the fruit retail business depended on credit from suppliers. United Fruit quickly rotted on the vine. Through the thirties David and Marco concentrated on keeping the Quality Fruit Shop alive.

A remarkable number of the early merchants in the Market were Sephardic Jews, descendants of Jews who settled in the eastern Mediterranean after being driven from Spain by Ferdinand and Isabella in 1492. Most of the Sephardim who reached Seattle came from the Island of Rhodes, south of Turkey, or from the islands and littoral of the Sea of Marmara, which before the First World War was a Turkish lagoon, though parts were claimed by Greece. These Jews spoke Turkish, Greek and, among

themselves, Ladino, a Romance language deriving from Spanish with Hebraic overtones. They didn't speak Yiddish, which astonished the Ashkenazim from Eastern Europe and made some doubt their authenticity as Jews.

One local legend has it that early in the 1900s a Sephardi from Rhodes, reaching New York and finding it overcrowded, bought a train ticket for as far away as he could get. "Eight days of trickyricky" brought him to Seattle, which was just beginning to pave its streets and build houses on its cow pastures. Here was the sixth day of creation and the city of opportunity. "Come," he wrote the folks back home, and they came. By 1913, Seattle's Sephardic community, which by no means threatened to overwhelm the Scandinavians or the Japanese, let alone the Anglo-Saxons, was the second or third largest in the United States.

David Levy was one of the first to arrive. He was living in a small Turkish town on the Sea of Marmara in 1902 when a friend who came back from America in search of a wife told him he'd like Seattle. When David arrived after the long trip across the continent, he went immediately to the waterfront, breathed the salt air, and decided "it was just like Marmara. I felt good."

Levy worked in tailor shops until he found something saltier, a job selling fish in the Palace Fish Market. In 1922, he bought out the old City Fish Market on Pike Place that had been set up by the city during the First World War to help keep down fish prices. It had become just another commercial outlet, getting its fish not from the state hatcheries, but from

ABOVE: *Dr. Sussman's spectacles stared at generations of visitors, reminding some of* The Great Gatsby. *(City of Seattle)*

FACING PAGE: *Jacob Feinberg was among the Sephardic Jews who established themselves in the Market soon after it opened. He specialized in "second-hand fruit," buying produce verging on over-ripeness and retailing at rock-bottom prices.* (Seattle Times)

the wholesalers. Levy earned the nickname "Good Weight Dave," and, catering to the taste of the fish-eating folk from southeastern Europe, made City Fish a Market institution.

Albert Ovadia came to Seattle in 1906 from Magarrah in Egypt to join his father. The elder Ovadia was selling fish from a basket. He'd buy it on the waterfront and carry it up the hill to the residential district, because streetcar conductors wouldn't let him bring his unwrapped fish onto the cars. After a brief apprenticeship with his father, Albert began working in the Market, eventually becoming an owner.

Selemo Calvo and Jacob Pelicar were among the first Sephardic immigrants. They came in 1903 at the urging of a Greek fisherman and found their first lodging with him. Jacob Almeleh, arriving in 1920 from Rhodes, found work immediately in the produce business. Eventually he had his own stand, "right opposite the Liberty Theater," and after hours edited *Progress,* a newspaper dedicated to uniting the Sephardic community.

Jacob Feinberg, another Sephardic immigrant, came to America in 1908 and two years later, at the age of twenty-one, reached Seattle. In 1911, he found a job at the Pike Place Market, and two years later set up his own fruit stand in the Sanitary Market. "Those days, with $100 you could do something." It was an era when most housewives canned their own fruit and vegetables. Jake specialized in buying produce at the ragged edge of overripeness and selling it cheaply by the box. He'd visit Western Avenue in the morning, take options on boxes if they were still available for delivery in the afternoon, and hustle bargains to shoppers looking for before-closing markdowns. His favorite wholesaler was

Pacific Food. They appreciated him, too: "Sometimes they'd send up fruit without asking me, and I'd have to scramble." He paid the produce companies each Wednesday when they came to check the books. Jake's system worked well for all concerned, keeping tons of fruit from going to waste. During the depression, he branched out and offered dry goods at distress sale prices.

Not all the Jews in the Market sold produce. A generation of shoppers became familiar with an electric sign just below the Public Market sign on Pike. It depicted an owl wearing eyeglasses and proclaimed that Dr. Sussman's was the cheapest place in town to buy spectacles. Dr. Sussman, a short, bald man in a dark suit and rimless glasses, could be found in his lower-floor stall, either studying a newspaper or leaning into the showcase polishing the glasses that sold for $2.50 a pair.

Another denizen of the lower Market who dealt in improved vision was Madame Nora, ethnic origin uncertain. A small woman with dark hair that softly curled to the middle of her neck, she usually arrived at the Market wearing a leopard skin coat. Stall fourteen, her place of work, was named the Temple of Destiny. (A stall alongside, which served as a retiring room, was called the Temple of Destiny Annex, but if Madame Nora engaged in activities other than Egyptian sand divining, Indian psychic projection, and crystal gazing in a five-inch sphere of blue glass resting on a blue mirror supported by a red silk cushion, it escaped the attention of authorities.) Hollywood's World Famous Sensational Crystal Gazing Queen, as Nora styled herself, enhanced her reputation as a clairvoyant when she entered a football prediction pool and won a trip to the Rose Bowl.

Across the narrow aisle from Madame Nora's Temple was a stall where an elderly Chinese man sold herbs, ginseng, dried seahorses that were reputed to restore virility, seaweeds of alleged therapeutic potentials, and condiments of vague, unspecified purpose. He had more lookers than buyers, but eventually made enough money for passage home to China.

Carly Westcott, who came from Denmark as a child, was one of the few to open a successful new business during the depression. In 1931, she rented a stall at a very low price since it had no ceiling. She covered the open space with burlap, brought in her own tonsorial equipment, and proclaimed herself The Market Barbershop. Brisk, quiet, and friendly, a charming figure in a gray blouse, dark skirt, and starched apron, she attracted a regular clientele, some of her customers coming from as far as West Seattle. Impeccably neat herself, Carly was sorry for the shabbily dressed men who frequented the Market, so she offered a depression special for the down-but-not-out: for a dollar a month, she gave a shave every week and a haircut every other week. After getting spruced up, a man might visit Mrs. Meyer's Open Kitchen in the Municipal Market Building where a full meal, soup through dessert, could be had for fifteen cents.

Angelina Mustelo opened a small grocery in the Market in 1928 and her daughter, Mamie-Marie, clerked there. Among those

calling frequently at Mama Mustelo's was a young man newly arrived from Italy, Peter Ramond De Laurenti, who delivered bread for the French Bakery (later acquired by Giglio Gai). In 1930, Peter married Mamie-Marie. They later bought out Mama Mustelo, changed the name to De Laurenti's, and developed their grocery into one of the Market's greatest godsends to gourmets.

One did not have to be foreign-born to succeed on Pike Place. C. B. Strong and J. W. Dunn were native to the U.S. Indeed, Strong's father is said to have been the first professional seedsman in the West. Young Strong was the first of the Puget Sound seed merchants to sell in wholesale quantities to the valley and island farmers, and when some of them moved to the newly irrigated areas in eastern Washington, they kept ordering from him.

In 1916, C. B. Strong & Co. took space in the Silver Oakum Building, and J. W. Dunn joined the company. He had been managing a brewery in Spokane, but the state's adoption of Prohibition in 1914 forced him to find a new line of work. When they lost their lease in 1918, they put up a building of their own at 1912 Pike Place. When Strong died of bromide poisoning (it was thought he overdosed to relieve a migraine), the

---

FACING PAGE, ABOVE: *Madame Nora presided over the Temple of Destiny. An eclectic prophetess who practiced crystal gazing, Indian psychic projection, and Egyptian sand divining, she once won a trip to the Rose Bowl in a football pool.* (Seattle Times)

ABOVE: *Peter Ramond De Laurenti married the daughter of a woman who ran a small grocery in the Market. He transformed it into a high-quality, low-frills delight for gourmets.* (Seattle Times)

FACING PAGE, BELOW: *Time, and even a great fire, have brought little change.* (Photo by Mary Randlett, University of Washington Libraries, Special Collections, Mary Randlett collection.)

name of the company was changed to J. W. Dunn Seeds, but it maintained its old reputation as the leading wholesale seed dealer in the area.

Joe Ford, a native-born American of Scottish-Irish ancestry, was drawn to Seattle by the publicity about the Alaska-Yukon-Pacific Exposition of 1909. He went to work in the Market as a butcher in February 1911, and his most vivid memory was of horses, three abreast, pulling low-slung wooden wagons loaded with carcasses from the slaughterhouses up Western Avenue to the Market.

Joe worked first for Frye & Company's outlet, then at the Rainier Market. There were no showcases when he started. After cutting the meat, he would lay it out on the marble display slabs by the aisle. Flies were accepted, as were pools of blood. It was 1918 before showcases with ammonia refrigeration were installed. One of Joe's duties in the early days was to keep an eye on a well-dressed woman who wore a handsome cape with hooks in the lining on which she hung the bloody loot she snatched from displays.

Wages were eighteen dollars a week plus two dollars carfare when Joe started, with hours from before dawn until you got through (which could be as late as 10 or 11 P.M. on Saturdays when the shop had to be cleaned for the weekend). Joe often told of the time when his friend, Pete Murray, planned to leave early but found that a load of twenty calves scheduled for noon had arrived instead at 4 P.M. The boss said, "You can leave when you've skinned them." Pete said, "I'll be leaving at five." Joe said, "Bet you a buck you can't." Pete, a craftsman with the knife and cleaver, skinned the calves, took out the livers, split the carcasses, hung them, and was away at five with Joe's dollar. Joe said the show was worth the price.

Sometimes when Joe was through early, he would cross First Avenue to the Liberty Theater and sing while Oliver Wallace played the organ. He was paid two dollars an evening for lining out Scottish and Irish ballads in the intervals between movies. He always brought along a pound of kidneys for Lightning, the theater cat.

On Saturdays, wholesalers brought extra meat to the Market in mid-afternoon. Everything was supposed to be sold before closing, so Joe often used his rich baritone in an auctioneer's sing-song: "What'll you give me? What'll you give me? How about a dollar? Four bits? Two bits? What'll you pay?" One Saturday afternoon he was chanting the praises and prices of beef slabs at the Washington Market when a young policeman, new to the beat, informed him that auctions were illegal. Arrested and taken to jail, Joe had to post fifty dollars bail. When the case came up in police court the charges were dropped. Nobody in the city attorney's office could find an ordinance against singing in the Market.

Over the years Joe worked for many shops, but during the depression, wages slid from the good times high of sixty-five dollars a week plus bonus to forty dollars a week plus five dollars expenses, so he quit and went into business for himself. As his own boss, Joe set out to end some of the practices he had observed during his years as an employee. Working through the Retail Meat Dealers Association, he helped draw up an ordinance requiring all butchers working at registered markets to be licensed. The applicant had to pass a written examination, an oral examination, and a health examination. During the same period, the council adopted an ordinance, the first in the nation, requiring compulsory grading of meat. The reforms were effective—so much so that some of the meat markets Joe Ford least admired moved out of town.

The Pike Place Market of the depressed thirties and prewar forties—the Byzantium on Elliott Bay with its mixture of races and array of products, a melting pot of Old World antagonisms and New World accommodations, a medley of contradictions pressed together in a container of wood and concrete, then pressured by the economy into accepting each other—was recorded by the region's foremost artist.

Mark Tobey had known the Market in an earlier period. The son of a Wisconsin carpenter, with little formal training in painting other than Saturday classes at the Chicago Art Institute, Tobey came to Seattle from New York in 1922. He was thirty-two years old, a refugee from a failed marriage and unsuccessful attempts to earn a living as portraitist, caricaturist, and magazine illustrator. Nellie Cornish, the impecunious impresario of Seattle arts, gave him a job teaching at the Cornish School, and somebody took him to the Market.

I walked down this fabulous array of colors and forms. So many things are offered for sale—plants to be replanted; ropes of all kinds; antiques; Norwegian pancakes made by an old sea captain, to be eaten on one of four stools on the sidewalk looking in. I hear the calls to buy— "Hey, you, come over here for the best tomatoes in the Market." Across the street are open shops under long burnt-orange-colored awnings.

BELOW: *Prohibition drove J. W. Dunn out of the brewery business in Spokane, but he caught on with C. B Strong & Co., which sold seeds. When the owner died, J. W. took over and renamed the business for himself. We see him, enthroned on bales, reigning over a growth industry. (Courtesy of Jerry Foster)*

The surface fascinated him, but Tobey did not immerse himself in the Market during the twenties. He was too busy finding himself and his art. He felt the pull of the Orient in the pulse of Pacific tides and wondered what the West would be like if it had been as closely tied to China and Japan as the eastern seaboard was to Europe. He learned about Chinese calligraphy from Teng Kuei, a student at the University of Washington. He responded to the rhythms of Salish weaving and Haida carving. And he found among Seattle social leaders patrons who purchased his works and brought him students for private instruction. (Patrons he certainly needed: the Cornish School charged students two dollars a session for his classes, of which he received eighty cents. There were four enrolled in his first class.)

Tobey was only intermittently in Seattle during the 1920s. He scraped together enough money to get to France in 1925 and early the following year went on to the Near East to visit the shrines of the Baha'i faith, to which he had become a convert in 1918. Returning to Seattle in 1927, he alternated teaching at Cornish with visits to New York and Chicago.

When the depression further undercut the Cornish school's shaky financial foundation, Tobey accepted a teaching assignment at Dartington Hall, 200 miles north of London, in Devonshire. The appointment was for six months, but Tobey stayed seven years at the progressive school. There he came to know Aldous Huxley, Rabindranath Tagore, Pearl Buck, Rudi Shankar, and other artists, many of whom shared his mystic bent. In 1934, the patrons of Dartington Hall made it possible for Tobey to visit the Far East and spend a month in a Zen monastery in Kyoto.

Tobey was briefly in Seattle in 1935 in connection with a one-man show, his first,

at the Seattle Art Museum. He returned to England by way of New York. Soon after getting back to Devonshire, while still thinking of Japan, he made a tracery of white calligraphic lines on a field of brown with small objects, mostly blue, caught in the mesh. Looking at the completed picture, he realized he had created a concept not of Kyoto, but of his impression of the Great White Way, "Broadway, with all the people caught in the lights." As he remembered it later, he completed two more Manhattan impressions within the week. In all three, the eye is carried through space by white-line tracery. *Broadway Norm*, *Broadway*, and *Welcome Hero* (also called *In the 1920s*) established Tobey's breakthrough into a new personal style synthesizing cubism and calligraphy.

Tobey came back to Seattle in 1938 on a six-month assignment with a Works Progress Administration art project, but the outbreak of war kept him here until progress drove him away in the fifties. A mature artist working his way deeper into the style that was to win him international attention, he took the Market to heart and his sketchpad to the Market.

Always possessed of a jackdown interest in objects that reflected their culture, a man for whom a trip through a five-and-ten could be "sheer exhilaration," he found in the Market a cornucopia of material. His friend Nancy Wilson Ross wrote of his delight in visiting "all sorts of special little shops where you can get Chinese rice, begonias, old copies of *Scientific American*, phonograph records from Siam, or Mt. Rainier painted on velvet."

The Market offered deeper pleasures. His Baha'i faith taught that "all humanity whether it be in the East or in the West may be connected through the bond of this divine affection; for we are all waves of one sea." In the Market, Tobey saw the

races of man mingled as the ocean mixes the waters of the rivers of the world.

In 1939 and 1940, he spent days on end in the Market, sketching produce, bric-a-brac, aisles, storefronts, architectural detail. But most of all in this period, which preceded his total immersion in abstraction, he sketched the people. In the introduction to his wonderful *The World of a Market,* Tobey wrote:

> Gathered in small groups like islands in the constant stream of people are the men for whom the Market is more than a place of gathering, almost a home. They live in furnished rooms and rundown hotels, some of them habitues of Skid Road at night and the Market in the day. From the many faces I picked out one man as someone I would like to know. He had looked at me with friendly eyes—I felt he knew me, so why not speak? "What is your lineage?" But I did not

expect the answer I got. "Adam and Eve, just like you my son."

I ran into my friend again. It was summer, and he was wearing a tropic helmet topped with a small carved wooden duck. His long, yellow-white hair was piled inside. His beard, starting around his eyes, flowed down almost to his waistline. "Come to my studio and let me paint you," I said. "You are an artist, why don't you paint your impression?" I made no further comment. He was a king of the Market.

In brown and black ink on pads of Chinese paper, Tobey sketched them,

---

ABOVE: *Mark Tobey was a master but not yet famous when he returned to paint for the Works Progress Administration. He haunted the Market, sketching everything, then returned to his studio to merge the fragments with major statements.* (Seattle Times, *March 17, 1946*)

though against absolute emptiness—a big blue space, a vacuum.'" Many of these sketches have been gathered in *The World of a Market*. They show three men in rumpled overcoats gathered to talk, a woman seen from behind holding a shopping bag, a man scavenging a barrel, a woman staring into a cup of coffee, a man reading a newspaper as he walks, and Joe Desimone, mustached, balding, standing at attention, a ruler greeting guests to his realm.

Back in his studio in the University District, he worked up these impressions, painting in tempera an aproned fishmonger in front of City Fish with a view up to the lighted arcade. In ink wash and tempera he recorded the odd angles of Frank Goodwin's architecture, the alley between the Economy Market and Pike Street, shoppers crowded into the arcade between the GG stalls and Lowell's Cafe, a vendor's table under a green-hooded lamp, the arcade as seen from Pike Place with wooden produce boxes stacked along the street side of the Market Building, a man reaching out gently as if to stroke a box of squash.

Tobey's sketches, and his time among the stalls, led to his major artistic statements about the Market, paintings dated between 1941 and 1945. Done in various media—oil, gouache, and tempera—and titled, *Time Off, Farmer's Market, Rummage, Point Five–Vertical, Working Man,* and *E Pluribus Unum*, they reflect the Market, the city that created it, and the period.

Opinions differ as to which is best. Roger Sale, in *Seattle: Past to Present*, favors *Rummage*, "one of the really great Tobeys, grander and more elusive than the others. The background, as usual, is very dark, and, as usual, the white line sets it in motion; but here the white line is itself in the background so that the objects emerge from it and are connected by it,

these men whom Nancy Wilson Ross described as "the tide-borne fragments of humanity, men from flophouses and dumps, thin men in bizarre garments, standing always, as Tobey once put it, 'as

and the motion of Market is a network in which the objects are fixed. The eye is kept moving, but is allowed to dwell on the objects: on the chair tilted at an odd angle—it is being discarded and will be sold soon; on the bust of a woman modeling a brassiere, on her feathered hat; on the cowboy next to her, who could be looking at her, but perhaps his eye is like ours and is going down an alley to a sign with letters that may be Japanese, or up to a stark hunched figure brooding at a bar counter."

Others prefer *E Pluribus Unum* with its obvious theme of the multitude merging into a unity. The figures of a bearded man, a boy, and a young woman share a heavily laden table set against a background of the Market throng and an infinity of lights and banners. Few would dispute Sale's conclusion that "In *Rummage*, and in the whole Market series, one has Tobey's Seattle, and for all the loneliness and pain to be found there, it is a city one would have liked to have lived in."

Chapter 6 | JOE DESIMONE, THE PATRIARCH OF PIKE PLACE

The Market Mark Tobey captured in oil and tempera, Joe Desimone captured in title. One of Tobey's sketches shows Joe, big, bald, and be-mustached, leaning forward deferentially like an overweight head waiter. The sketch reflects an aspect of the man, not the essence. It was easy to be mistaken about Joe. A *National Geographic* article in February 1933 was exact in its description of the Market atmosphere—"vegetables temptingly displayed to attract shoppers. The bouquet behind the lettuce tray consists of 'flowers' fashioned from turnips, beets and other roots and mounted in garden greens"—but it called Desimone "the mustached Belgian proprietor."

Giuseppe Desimone was born in 1880 on a farm about forty miles east of Naples in Avellino province of southern Italy. A big-boned, willful youngster with scant formal education, he was intelligent enough to see little future in turning the fertile but waterless volcanic dust of a tenant farm with hoe and plow. At fifteen, after a quarrel with his father about farming methods, he left home. At seventeen, having earned forty dollars in two years, he stowed away on a ship bound for America.

He was put ashore on Ellis Island in 1897, almost penniless, without peers, without English. An official asked for his passport. He stammered something in the dialect of Campagna and the man thoughtfully turned his back. Taking the hint, Desimone fled. For the rest of his life he admired obliging officials.

Desimone learned enough English to get around the working world of the immigrant, anglicized his given name to Joe, and found a job in New York at eighty-three cents a day. Some months later an uncle wrote him about the damp glories of the Puget Sound low country where "vegetables grow like weeds." Next stop, the Italian community in Rainier Valley.

Powerfully built, accustomed to hard work and long hours, knowledgeable about farming, Desimone had no difficulty catching on as a hired hand for the Vacca family, but he lusted for land of his own. He took extra jobs, saved every penny, dreamed only of a farm and a deed. One day, on the way to a friend's place to borrow a plow, he met a dark-haired girl who happened to be from his native village. Her name was Assunta and she was sixteen. Their courtship was brief.

Desimone leased a farm in Georgetown, working it in the early morning and late evening. He saved enough to lease a second farm at South Park, with an option to buy. He quit his job and ran both farms, working each day until ready to drop, Assunta beside him in the fields until their first child, Peter, was born. They raised truck—corn, potatoes, lettuce, celery, carrots, beets, turnips, onions, radishes, cauliflower, cabbage, beans, and peas—the usual produce of the valley farms.

They lived on the rented Georgetown farm until a soap company from San Francisco bought the land. Then they moved to the South Park farm on which they had an option. Joe figured he'd have the money for the down payment when the 1909 harvest was in, but the Duwamish flooded, sweeping away outbuildings, ruining equipment, destroying the crops in the field. "My wife, she cry," Joe recalled, "but it make me mad. I borrow money and buy the little farm anyway. No water she is going to stop me."

He had a peasant's obsession with land, the landless farmer's lust for ownership. "All wealth she come from the land," he would shout, waving his arms. "A good piece of land, she is worth any store or even gold field in alla world." And he was willing to work for what he wanted. On a typical day he would get up between 2 and 3 A.M., feed the horse, put on the harness, lead the horse to the already loaded cart of produce, hitch it up, and travel the gravel road along the Duwamish into town. He'd get a stall at Westlake or, later, at Pike Place, work till closing, and start home, arriving around 9 P.M.—in time to do a little work in the field, check on the produce, unload the wagon, and put in fresh produce before dinner and bed.

FACING PAGE: *Joe Desimone, who succeeded the Goodwins as the most influential figure in the Market, was not only self-made, he was self-invented. In this 1915 picture, he spelled his name and dated his company in a way he later changed. (City of Seattle)*

He pumped his earnings back into the farm, into ways of marketing produce, into more land. The South Park farm spread to cover fifteen acres. There was a ten-room farmhouse and a bunkhouse for the eight or nine men who were hired to work the crops in the growing season. For years, Assunta cooked three meals a day for the hands; later Joe hired a Filipino cook, since most of the men were from the Philippines. Everyone in the family worked the land. The children weeded. Assunta took green onions the men brought to the barn and tied them into bunches with strands of bunch grass, two or three hundred bunches a day. Joe borrowed money, bought a swamp near the Duwamish, dug drainage canals that transformed muck fifteen feet deep into prime farmland. Later he leased the reclaimed soil to tenants—most of them Italian or Japanese immigrants, repaid the cost of development out of rents, then looked for more swamps.

In 1915, he bought two Model T Ford trucks and, styling himself Desimone and Brothers, set up a delivery route to Seattle groceries including Augustine and Kyre, Madrona Grocery, Harron Brothers on Capitol Hill, and Dod Brothers. There were many others. This was the era of the neighborhood grocery. The Desimone service continued into the late twenties with his sons, Richard and Mondo, sometimes serving as drivers. (Mondo then developed a route of his own, serving the Olympic Hotel, Bolt's Restaurant, Rippey's, York Lunch, Yale Lunch, and groceries on Olive Way, Broadway, Capitol Hill, and Madison Park, with Providence Hospital as the last stop.)

When the Goodwins opened the GG stalls in 1922, Joe was the only producer ready to pungle up seventy-five dollars a month to rent one. When Arthur Goodwin bought the Market Company from his uncles in 1925, Joe bought some stock. When Arthur's friend Walter Taylor sold his interest in 1927, Joe bought it, becoming the second largest stockholder in, and vice president of, Pike Place Public Markets, Inc.

All the while, he kept planting most of his earnings in land. By 1928, Joe owned more than seventy acres of farmland in the South Park area, as well as scattered holdings throughout the county. He was a leader in the Italian community, a *padrone* among the *campesino* who worked for him, who leased his land, who came to him for advice and loans and introductions. He was a political leader as well, the friend of county commissioners and city councilmen, a man who could deliver votes as well as baskets of fruits and vegetables.

He played the role of peasant Falstaff: a huge man—320 pounds at one time—he favored a costume of calf-high boots, white shirt, and bib overalls. He avoided putting on airs as he avoided the evil eye. A fellow of boisterous spirit and native wit, he was determined to excel in hospitality while refusing to admit that he had become wealthy.

Assunta was still tying onions in the vegetable shed on the South Park farm when a business associate of Joe's convinced her that she and her husband had enough money to remodel the farmhouse. At the party to celebrate the remodeling, Joe wore his overalls as he poured wine for city councilmen, Pike Place Market Company's officials, and the *campesino*; supervised the passing of platters of meatballs, ravioli, macaroni, antipasto, white radishes, and French bread; all the time thundering commands to "Eat! Eat! Eat more! Come-a on, drink. Drinka your vino!" When the guests had eaten to the bursting point, Joe circled the table with the main course, a huge turkey stuffed with almonds and cauliflower buds prepared to look like cream-colored roses. "Eat! Eat! Drinka your vino!"

He professed to have no respect for book learning, especially after the stock market crash when he saw men who had put all their money in stocks rather than land reduced to sudden poverty. "What's the use the educate?" he would ask, adding that he could write nothing more than his own name (which he signed with rococo flourish).

Those, like Arthur Goodwin, who worked with him learned, however, that he could study a contract and detect its soft spots as surely as a corporation lawyer. Goodwin discovered that when the big fellow who lubbered around in overalls looked at a proposed agreement and said, "Arturo, I don't like this," the company attorney was likely to agree.

Joe was litigious, involved in more than twenty suits in King County Superior Court, some of which went to the State Supreme Court. Though usually generous and jovial, he could be harsh; in one court action, a former employee accused Desimone of chasing him with a horsewhip. He was not reluctant to use his position, whether it was to reward a politician with baskets of cabbage or to see that an enemy got unfavorable treatment from an official. Willard Soames and the Associated Farmers, who had fought the Pike Place Public Market Company over the GG stalls, opened a paper bag business in the Market. Woe to the Italian farmer who bought Will's bags!

Dueling with lawyers in court gave Joe the opportunity to play the farm boy. When an attorney asked him about his reputation for ruthlessness, he replied, "We farmer, we have to work, not like you fellows that look over the books, and furnish everything. They say a lot of things.

ABOVE: *Mark Tobey's sketch catches Joe at his most Falstaffian. (Mark Tobey,* To Desimonia, *1940, Pen and Brown Ink on tan Japanese paper, 222 mm x 144 mm, Dr. Harold Joachim Purchase Fund, G26071, The Art Institute of Chicago)*

I pay no attention." On another occasion he explained his wealth: "I work hard. I save alla time. I get a little land here and a little land there. I have lots of trouble. But alla time I persist. I save and I wait and I persist."

He feuded with some neighbors. When solvency increased his influence in the early thirties, he persuaded county road crews to fill Mill Creek and Hamm Creek with dredge spoils from the Duwamish to the displeasure of the Seattle Dahlia Gardens, among others. They found their water supply cut off by Joe's improvements. They sued the county and Joe for loss of water rights and destroyed crops, won a restraining order, damages, and a new culvert. Bitterness over the dispute and other self-serving accommodations he reached with pliable officials lasted for years. But so did memories of his generosity with those who did not cross him.

"Joe, Joe was my friend. But those others, American people, I don't know," said Antonio Ditore, one of the Italian farmers who rented stalls in the wet row. "Joe, he tells me, 'If you need money, I give you money if you want.' You didn't find people like him very easy. He was a good heart. Desimone he was a besta man I know."

Mrs. George, who managed the Leland Hotel for a time, felt the same way. "Joe Desimone was good to everybody . . . I'm from farm people too. He helped a lot of people. He took Italians in, helped them when they couldn't speak. I will never forget him. I always put Mr. Desimone in my prayers."

Joe's peasant faith in land as power and his "alla time saving" led to the Desimones' supplanting the Goodwins as the dominant family at Pike Place. When Arthur bought out his uncle Frank in 1925, he purchased the company and its leases, but the land remained under the control of his uncle, who established the Pike Place Investment Company to hold title to the real estate. Frank and Arthur made an oral agreement that the Pike Place Public Market Company would receive $121.19 a month to supervise the Outlook Market Building, while the Pike Place Investment Company would reimburse the Market Company for lighting, advertising, and repair bills. The system worked smoothly as long as business was good. After the crash in '29, the Market Company continued to make its monthly payments to the Investment Company, but no reimbursements for expenses came the other way.

By 1931, the Market Company was in serious trouble. Everything that could be mortgaged was mortgaged and second-mortgaged. In October, Arthur wrote a painful letter to his uncle Ervin, who handled rent collections and other bookkeeping matters for the investment company:

Dear Ervin:

We find that we can no longer pay the monthly salary of $90 per month for the collection of rents at the market. I am therefore notifying you that beginning November 1, we shall have to discontinue services in this connection.

As you know, this has been brought about by our not being able to collect from your office the money that has been due for us for some time past.

We have been badly crippled by not being able to collect these amounts from you, and find that we will not be able to pay our taxes this coming November because of it.

We wish that you would please make every effort to return at least

part of this money to us so that we can keep in good standing with the bondholders and stockholders of this company. We have all felt here that if we could keep this enterprise above water during these times, that it could be used as a refuge and safe harbor in times of need.

Sincerely yours,
Arthur E. Goodwin

There was no response. The depression deepened. In November 1932, Arthur decided that the only way to pay the back taxes would be for him to sell some of his stock. Joe suggested a friend who had ready cash, I. A. "Paul" Caraco. Arthur hesitated. The sale would involve only three percent of the stock but it would leave him with less than a controlling interest. Joe assured him, "Arturo, I will vote with you."

The sale was made. Goodwin remained president of the Pike Place Public Market Company—true to his word, Joe did not vote against him—but Joe became the key figure in decision-making. By 1933 he held just over half of the 3,000 shares in the company.

In 1933, the Market Company filed

ABOVE: *The Desimone era in the Market ended when Seattle bought out the Desimone property, but the bridge over Western Avenue bears the name of the peasant boy who for a time reigned over Pike Place. (Photo by Mary Randlett)*

suit against the Investment Company to recover the money due for expenses in running the Outlook Market—$7,101 plus interest. Arthur faced his uncle, friend, and mentor, Frank Goodwin, in court. The judge awarded the Market Company $4,393.44, the balance of the debt being barred by the statute of limitations.

This was a painful time for Arthur Goodwin. He was in effect an employee of the company he had founded. Though business improved, he lost his love for the paneled office with its tile fireplace and huge conference desk. He had other interests: he was president of the Carbon Dioxide Company, a dry ice manufacturing firm in Salt Lake City, and vice president of the Fulton Petroleum Company in Montana. He was much in demand as a consultant on market business (his book, *Markets: Public and Private*, published in 1929, remained the bible in its field). He took every opportunity to be out of town.

Joe brought in Paul Caraco as assistant manager to handle Arthur's duties during his absences. Caraco took to the manager's desk as if it had been carpentered for him. He opened Goodwin's mail even when Goodwin was in town, gave orders, and made decisions even if Goodwin was no farther away than the restroom, making it clear that the company president ranked as spear-carrier in the new order.

In 1941 Goodwin sold his remaining stock in the company to Desimone. He also sold his Seattle home, Goodwin Manor. An era had ended. Joe Desimone became in name as well as practice the president of the company, the biggest man in the Market.

The black lettering on the milky glass of the office door was formal—Pike Place Public Markets, Inc. and Pike Investment Co.—but the door was always open. The president, usually in overalls, sat at

Goodwin's old desk behind the wooden partition separating the business counter from executive space. There was an interoffice phone but he didn't use it. Joe could always make himself heard. "Rosie, get me a check." "Rosie, get me Paul." "Rosie, get a sandwich."

He was utterly accessible. Anybody could see Joe without an appointment, be he bank president, wholesaler, a farmer needing a loan, or a shopper who thought he'd been short-weighted. Most of the tenants loved him, the exceptions being those who wanted their stalls improved. Old tenants such as David Mossafer volunteered testimonials:

> See, those Desimones, finest people in the world. They got one policy, never kick anybody out. You got little place there, you can stay there as long as you do the right thing for the people, for yourself, and for the Market. They never, never take anybody out. For instance, you pay $200 a month and somebody comes along and says to them, "I give you $500." If you give him $1000 a month he won't rent to you. "We don't raise the rent. We don't operate that way." That's the policy of the office.

There was another side to this policy of looking after the old-timers. The Market was a family business and family business was private business. Problems were never discussed with outsiders. Nor were expenditures made casually. A memorandum by a city official who dealt with the Desimones remarked that they ran the Market according to an old country principle, "to maintain frugally what one has and not to expand."

Joe might have been slow with a dollar for improvements, but he was quick with advice for everybody. He would

pause on the sidewalk to shout at a vendor to water his flowers, then climb in his Ford truck, double-park in front of Seattle First National Bank, and go in to bawl out a vice president about bad advice on an investment—advice he hadn't taken anyway.

The glory years of Joe's reign ended abruptly. In 1942, overweight and overactive, he suffered a stroke. Joe never resumed active command of the business, though he did come to the office from time to time to look in on his son, Richard, who was now running things for the family. Knowing from firsthand experience the perils to continuity of divided ownership of a company, he inserted in his will a clause preventing any of his heirs from selling part of their Market stock: "Control of the Market should be centered in one place and it shall therefore be arranged, if possible, that all of the stock in the market owned by the marital community composed of my wife and myself be placed in the hands of my Trustee, exchanging, if necessary, other of my property for such shares of stock as my wife would otherwise be entitled to as her part of the community estate."

One afternoon late in 1945, Arthur Goodwin and his wife drove out to visit Joe on his farm. They found him wrapped in blankets, his face pale. He had suffered another stroke and knew he was dying, but he was glad they had come. "Arturo, I'm sorry things I did to you. I make trouble for you. I very sorry, Arturo, I'm a very sorry. I know now what happened."

A few days later, on January 4, 1946, Joe Desimone died, but his legend lives on at the Pike Place Public Market. The Joe Desimone Bridge spans Western Avenue; on a wall in the farmers' arcade, the city has placed a plaque dedicated to him; and in the stalls and shops of the Market the story is told and retold of the farm boy who persisted and became president of the company and King of Pike Place.

ABOVE: *A plaque in the farmers' arcade on Pike Place honors Joe Desimone—and raises a question among his admirers. How did they ever get Joe in a suit? (Photo by Mary Randlett)*

Chapter 7 | Empty Stalls

On November 2, 1941, advertisements in the Sunday papers featured pictures of smiling Japanese farmers at the Pike Place Public Market. Under the photos were captions stressing the quality and low cost of the produce the Japanese brought to the Market. One said, "Shop Here for Thrift as prices are always lower." Another, "Shop Here for Health as vegetables are always fresh and you get a full measure of health-giving vitamins and minerals."

Five weeks later to the day, Pearl Harbor was bombed and the Japanese Americans at the Market found themselves objects of suspicion and hatred. It was not a new experience.

The Japanese had been part of the Market scene from the start. Unlike the Chinese, who began coming to the West Coast during the California gold rush of the 1850s and were imported in such numbers during the building of the transcontinental railroads in the 1860s and 1870s that they became the object of organized hostility, the Japanese were relative latecomers and not numerous. This did not prevent their falling heir to the epithet, "the yellow peril."

The Census Bureau recorded 55 Japanese residents in the U.S. in 1870, only 148 a decade later. The passage of Chinese exclusion acts in 1882 and 1888, and clauses in the U.S.-China treaty of 1894, prohibited the immigration of Chinese laborers to the U.S. Corporations seeking disciplined, industrious, low-cost labor began to encourage Japanese immigration. By 1910, there were some 72,000 Japanese in the country; fewer than one in a thousand. Of these, 12,929 lived in Washington. They constituted 1.1 percent of the state's population.

Many Japanese had been brought to Washington under contract to work in the lumber camps, where they often operated as segregated units with separate bunkhouses and messes. Others were employed in mining or railroad construction, but nearly all felt the appeal of what, after Japan, seemed almost vacant land. A farm meant independence.

The Washington State Constitution, adopted in 1889 during a period of anti-Chinese agitation, had a clause forbidding foreign ownership of land, but it was possible for an alien to rent farmland, and sometimes to buy it in the name of a trusted citizen. This the Japanese did. Their experience was in truck farming rather than grains, so most settled in western Washington rather than in the wheat country across the Cascades.

FACING PAGE: *A* Seattle Times *photographer pictured the stalls the day after evacuation. Not until the Japanese were forcibly transplanted to concentration camps in 1942 did Seattle realize how important they were to the city's food supply.*

ABOVE AND BELOW: *Planting lettuce and harvesting berries near the White River. (Photos by Frank Natsuhara)*

Vegetables travel poorly, so the farms were concentrated on the outskirts of existing cities, especially the two largest, Tacoma and Seattle.

Skilled at making small plots productive in their island homeland, notably hardworking, accustomed to family-sized enterprises, they made the suburban valleys beautiful as well as fruitful. Their success aroused the hostility of some competitors, and their concentration in the Puget Sound area fueled the agitation by making the Japanese seem more numerous than they really were.

Agitation against the Chinese had stressed that they would work for low wages, thus, it was argued, driving the wage scale for whites "down to the coolie level." Complaints against the Japanese alleged they were so industrious they could sell at lower prices than their rivals and eventually monopolize land God had intended for whites.

An early Japanese farmer in the White River Valley remembered:

We had a very hard time with poor whites. In the second summer I spent in America, an American farmer proposed that we weed his carrot gardens by contract at a very low price. We refused to work except by the day, so he hired white children in Kent who worked well while the boss was watching, but as soon as he was away played on the farm, pulled up many carrots and left weeds in their places. On his return the boss discharged the children and hired Japanese, thus displeasing the people of Kent, who said, Japs take jobs away from Americans, so let's kick them out. After that trouble it was dangerous for us to go into Kent because we were targets for jeers, sticks and stones whenever we appeared on the streets.

The growing number of Japanese farmers selling produce at the Pike Place Market was a cause of concern. On the wet row, they sometimes outnumbered whites four to one. In 1910, a city council committee studied a proposed ordinance giving American citizens preference over aliens in the assignment of stall space. The Japanese Consul in Seattle protested. The secretary of the Seattle Chamber of Commerce wrote to remind the councilmen that the Treaty of Commerce and Navigation between Japan and the United States promised there would be no discrimination against nationals resident in each other's country; therefore, any ban aimed at Japanese would apply equally to other aliens:

MR. PRESIDENT –

The Kent Washington Post of the American Legion respectfully invites you to be their guest at their second annual Lettuce Festival on June 22". 1935...

(Signed) –LETTUCE FESTIVAL COMMITTEE

The officers of this Chamber trust that under the circumstances your honorable committee will see the futility of attempting the enforcement of any such police regulation, which if enacted would apply not only to Japanese but the subjects of several other foreign nations, who are the most profitable tenants of some of the numerous land holders in King County, and who are a considerable factor in regulating prices in the markets of this city, thereby materially reducing the cost of living.

However unclear the "who" to whom the "whos" in the missive referred, the committee killed the proposed ordinance. The Japanese position in the Public Market remained strong enough to enable them to win acceptance of a 1914 request that stall assignment be returned to a straight lottery system rather than one they suspected was being manipulated by the Market Master to the advantage of the whites.

When Arthur Goodwin was invited to Vancouver, British Columbia, in 1922 to give advice on the way to run a public market, he was flat out in favor of letting the Asians grow what they could and sell what they could:

If your market is left to the few white farmers who are producing vegetables and green stuff it will never be filled. Not enough white men go into this work to keep it going. They cannot compete with the Oriental, who is willing to work longer hours and has a cheaper standard of living.

At Seattle and Portland, the Oriental farmers are very much in evidence in the markets. They grow the largest quantities of produce and know how to display and sell it. Here, I understand, most of your vegetable produce is grown by Orientals. If you would have a market teeming with business, where the produce of the farm may be bought fresh and clean every day, you must do as the markets of the neighboring cities have done and give the Oriental a place.

FACING PAGE: *Barred by law from acquiring real estate, immigrant Japanese worked as tenant farmers until their native-born children could get land of their own. Here the Ikeda family pick berries on a tenant farm along the White River. (Photo by Frank Natsuhara)*

ABOVE: *Japanese children, born American citizens, invited President Franklin D. Roosevelt to the Second Annual Lettuce Festival. (He couldn't make it.) (City of Seattle)*

I hold no brief for the Orientals but the market is established to provide fresh produce as cheaply as possible to the housewives. If it does not succeed in doing this it will be a failure.

Such local acceptance was a current counter to the tide. The State of Washington, under pressure from the resurgent Ku Klux Klan, adopted an alien land law measure aimed at blocking the leasing of farmland by aliens, as well as the practice the Japanese called *hakuji,* buying land in the name of a cooperative citizen. Then, in 1924, Congress passed a law effectively ending Asian immigration. Between 1920 and 1940 the Japanese population in Washington fell to 2,822, and the percentage of Washington residents who were Japanese fell from 1.3 percent to 0.8 percent.

With the small drop in actual numbers (but a one-third drop in percentage) of Japanese, talk of the Yellow Peril faded. There were, of course, ethnic slurs, and race might be mentioned in business

arguments, but it was possible, as Monica Sone has reported in her fine book, *Nisei Daughter,* to come to school age unaware of the importance others put on ethnic background; to come to December 7, 1941, unaware that there would be a question of allegiance in a war between Japan and the United States.

Then, Pearl Harbor—a moment fixed in the memory of a generation. For Sone, the Nisei, second generation, daughter of an Issei, immigrant, couple who ran a leased hotel on the Seattle waterfront, word came when a University of Washington student named Chuck burst into a choir rehearsal for the annual

ABOVE: *The Sanitary Public Market, with its street-level groceries and its garment shops on the upper floors, typified the Market mix until it was gutted by fire in December 1941. (King County Assessor's Office)*

FACING PAGE: *A workman found this picture of the Market burning in the basement of the Sanitary Market. (Pike Place Market Preservation and Development Authority)*

Christmas recital of Handel's *Messiah:* "Listen, everybody! Japan just bombed Pearl Harbor, in Hawaii! It's war." Sone recalled later:

An old wound opened up again, and I found myself shrinking inwardly from my Japanese blood, the blood of an enemy . . .

One girl mumbled over and over again, "It can't be, God, it can't be." Someone else was saying, "What a spot to be in. Do you think we'll be considered Japanese or Americans." A boy replied quickly, "We'll be Japs, same as always. But our parents are enemy aliens now, you know."

Courtney S. Payton was seated in his radio shop in the Sanitary Market Building eight days after Pearl Harbor when a series of muffled explosions brought him to his feet. Outside flames were shooting from the wall on the Pike Place side. Payton opened the door to the hall and was met with a wall of smoke. He dropped to his hands and knees and crawled to safety, the floor beneath him bouncing as stocks of matchboxes, vegetable oils, paper bags, and other dry goods exploded into flame. Out on First Avenue, the smoke was so thick that firemen answering the second and third alarms could hardly see the building. Autos parked on the street steamed when

BLIC MARKET
AT YOUR SERVICE
STREET CARS
TEL.
Ma. 5231
STALL 5-7-9
JOHNNIES
TARY MEAT
WHOLESALE & RETAIL
VICH

water fell on them. Power lines, showering sparks, fell in the street. Patrons at the Liberty Theater were evacuated into the alley as smoke poured into the building. Lightning, the theater's mascot, ran inside to escape the turmoil, but ushers rescued him. Nothing could save the Sanitary Market. It was gutted, though the adjoining structures were saved.

The fire had started on an awning, but the cause was never determined. Rumors spread that Japanese were involved, though why the Sanitary Market would be targeted was never explained. The mood in the stalls grew ugly. Japanese farmers wore pins declaring "I AM AN AMERICAN," but sales fell. Many automobile insurance companies canceled Japanese policyholders as bad risks. Some kept driving to the Market in uninsured cars, but others stayed on their farms waiting for they knew not what.

Rumors spread that Japanese would be relocated to concentration camps. Banks, afraid to risk loans to buy seed and fertilizer for crops that might not be harvested, cut off credit. President Roosevelt signed Executive Order No. 9066 authorizing the War Department to remove Japanese from such military areas as it saw fit, aliens and American-born Japanese alike—no matter how small the person's percentage of Japanese blood. General J. L. DeWitt declared western Washington, Oregon, all of California, and the southern half of Arizona to be a military area which must be cleared of Japanese. In March, General DeWitt

issued a ban on voluntary evacuations and imposed curfew and travel restrictions on all Japanese, while relaxing those on Germans and Italians.

The Reverend Dr. Daisuke Kitagawa was pastor of a small Methodist congregation in the White River Valley. Many of his Japanese parishioners sold fruit and vegetables at the Pike Place Market. He loved making his pastoral rounds during spring planting, when the valley was at its most beautiful, loved seeing "the smiling faces of boys and girls helping their parents in the gardens. I used to make all my pastoral calls right in the fields. From the middle of February on, wherever I went, I used to see men driving tractors and cultivating the land, the girls and women busy handling seedlings in the hothouses. The spring air, filled with the fragrance of all kinds of flowers, was vibrant with life."

The spring of 1942 was different. "When I drove around the valley, few people greeted me. The whole valley looked deserted. When I knocked at the kitchen door—only strangers who had to be formal went to the front door—I was greeted by voices filled with anxiety and fear. Toward the end of March we began to hear about one place after another in California having been given two weeks notice to get ready for mass evacuation. It was really deadly for the farmers to have to stay on their farms without doing anything. Every one of them would have been extremely happy to double efforts to produce had they been assured that they would be allowed to stay until after the harvest."

The failure of most Japanese to plant crops led to a new rumor: they were trying to sabotage the war effort by curtailing the food supply. Their isolation increased. No act of sabotage or plot to sabotage was ever confirmed, but the rumors swelled, undiminished by the fact

FACING PAGE: *The cause of the fire that swept the Sanitary Market was never determined, but the disaster happened only days after Pearl Harbor. Inevitably, rumor attributed it to Axis saboteurs. The Japanese were powerless to combat wartime prejudice. (Pike Place Market Preservation and Development Authority)*

that the Army decided it was not necessary to evacuate Japanese from Hawaii.

In April, Seattle's Japanese received orders to pack up and get out:

Dispose of your homes and property. Wind up your business. Register the family. One seabag of bedding, two suitcases of clothing allowed per person. People in District #1 must report at 8th and Lane Street, 8 A.M. on April 28.

They had less than a month to find someone to take over their leases, to dispose of personal property they could not take with them, and they were in no position to drive bargains. They were lucky to get ten cents on the dollar. Much was given away to neighbors or abandoned.

Tom Iwasaki had purchased ten acres on the Duwamish in 1911, using a friendly white man as a front. When he had to leave, he could find no one to lease his farm, so turned his house over to a family, rent-free. When he returned in 1946 he found every pane in his greenhouses broken, seeds scattered, plants that had been growing when he left strangled at their stakes. His two sons were in the Army in Europe but his daughters spent two weeks helping him pick up broken glass. He expressed no bitterness when talking about it in 1975, at the age of ninety: "The internment camps were not so bad. They treated you well. At least you were protected from burning and looting. It was the people who were leasing who lost everything."

The order to move came on April 21:

All the Seattle Japanese will be moved to Puyallup by May 1. Everyone must be registered Saturday and Sunday between 8 A.M. and 5 P.M. They will leave next week in three groups, on Tuesday, Thursday and Friday.

It was an orderly evacuation. Seattle Japanese were taken, some by bus, others by train, to the Western Washington Fairgrounds in Puyallup. There they were held in wooden barracks surrounded by barbed wire, searchlights playing constantly around the grounds at night, soldiers with tommyguns watching them from towers. The concentration camp was called Camp Harmony. After several months the internees were relocated to permanent camps.

On May 6, 1942, six months after the November 2 advertisement that pictured Japanese farmers smiling across their array of cheap and healthy produce at the Market, the *Seattle Star* ran a two-column picture of the "new All-American Farmers' Row" at Pike Place. "Business is much, much better," the caption claimed. "An abundance of clean, fresh and appetizing farm produce is on hand as usual and will be on hand right along, the farmers say. Since the Japanese evacuation began, said I. A. Caraco, vice president and general manager of the Market, there hasn't been a vacancy. The Market in general is enjoying an excellent increase in business because white patrons like to buy from white farmers. Cooperation between patrons and merchants is consequently much closer than it was."

Nonetheless, the number of farmer-seller licenses issued for the Market dropped from 515 in 1939 to 196 in 1943. More than one-third of the evacuated Japanese never returned to Seattle, and only a few farmers from the valley recovered their land and returned to Pike Place. Old-timers say the Market has never been the same.

FACING PAGE: *Many Japanese were forced to close shop before the evacuation. After May 1, the New Management signs were everywhere. (both photos* Seattle Times)

Chapter 8 | FULL ROOMS

Among the Japanese sent to Camp Harmony in the spring of 1942 were Rosuke and T. K. Kodama and their four children. The Kodamas held the lease on the Outlook Hotel that loomed above Western Avenue at the foot of Pike Street. Built in 1909, the big wooden building commanded a magnificent view of Elliott Bay and the Olympics—a fact exploited by the architect, who liberally bedecked the fifty-seven room edifice with bay windows, some outlined with stained glass. Time had dimmed the interior of the Outlook, if not the view, and under the Kodamas the hotel catered to frugal workmen and the elderly.

Nellie Curtis, who bought out the Kodamas' lease in the bargain counter days of the evacuation, had a different clientele. Nellie was a well-known Seattle businesswoman, a professional in the oldest profession. She was also known to authorities across western Canada and the United States as Zella Curtis, Zella Nightengale, Yeta Curtis, Edna Douglas, Mrs. Dennis Kane, Yeta Solomon, Kitty Solomon, Mrs. Ray Finkle, Zella Kana, and Nellie Gray. She specialized in running very orderly disorderly houses.

Born (she alleged) Zella Nightengale, married at eighteen, Nellie and her sister, generally called Ida Klein, took off for Canada to make their fortunes. That they did. First operating rooming houses with an exceptionally high tenant turnover, then running licensed houses of prostitution in Swift Current, Saskatchewan, and a commodious establishment near the mine-head in Kimberley, B.C., they did nicely. After ten prosperous years providing recreation, if not rest, for libidinous lumberjacks, cowboys, and miners, and squirreling away the profits south of the border in bank vaults from Milwaukee to Portland, Nellie could greet the depression with $150,000 worth of equanimity.

Times were worse in western Canada than in the States, so in 1931 Nellie came down to Seattle, took up residence in the Garden Court apartments, and made a study of local opportunity. Combining the traditions of frontier town, seaport, and logging community—all places with large populations of transient males—Seattle, in spite of occasional spasms of morality, was an open town. By tacit agreement with constituted authority, prostitution was tolerated south of Yesler Way, a thoroughfare for which the Reverend Mark Matthews, an authority on Seattle sin, provided a classic description: "Yesler Way was once a skid road down which logs were pushed to Henry Yesler's sawmill on the waterfront. Today it is a skid road down which human souls go sliding to hell."

Nellie knew better than to locate in such disreputable surroundings. Not only would competition be concentrated nearby, she knew that whenever things got hot and politics demanded that the city be temporarily chaste, she'd have to close along with the other operators. After a two-year survey, she moved into the Camp Hotel on the second floor of a two-story building at First and Virginia, the north end of the Pike Place Market area. There she stayed for eight relatively uneventful years, subject to one yearly raid and $100 fine, but hardly harassed by vigorous law enforcement. The neighboring Paris Rooms attracted more notoriety. An earnest young city councilman, Arthur Langlie, paid them a well-chaperoned visit and reported seeing one girl sitting on a davenport, another playing solitaire. The councilman and his companion were invited to see other rooms, but declined. The Paris eventually closed, but Langlie went on to be mayor.

The Camp survived a similarly innocuous exposé that was made and testified to by the owner of a local tire company, Floyd Franklin Thompson. He told a city council hearing on vice about climbing the flight of stairs off First Avenue and, after being inspected through a peephole, being admitted to Nellie's establishment:

There was a colored matron that met us. She asked us—pardon me, I should have said this was Stanley Anderson and myself that went into this place. She showed us into a waiting room, where there was a davenport, two davenports, chairs, a very nicely furnished place, and had quite

FACING PAGE: *Nellie Curtis is remembered for her roomful of hats, her drawers full of currency, and her genteel management of the last of Seattle's big-time bawdy-houses.* (Los Angeles Times)

a homey atmosphere about it. She showed us into a waiting room, and we sat there and we talked for perhaps five minutes and I suggested that we go. So we got up and we started out of this reception room. And the lady in charge met us, I imagine she was about thirty-eight years old, and quite attractive, and by that time one of the girls was through so she came over. They wore, the girls wore shorts with very tricky little blouses of some kind, very attractive. And this Stan Anderson knew the matron in charge, knew the woman that owned the place. He sold her a Cadillac, a $5,000 Cadillac, the year before. She paid cash for it. And so they talked. And they talked about business, and business seemed to be very good with her. And so we told her we would be back later.

Armed with this information, Seattle police got around to raiding the joint six years later, in July 1941. They arrested a young woman wearing silk pajamas in the living room. Their suspicions about her were deepened when they found in her purse a physician's card certifying that two days earlier she had been free of venereal infection. This was not overwhelming legal evidence that Nellie's girls were doing what they were doing and the case fizzled out in police court. Still, a raid was not Nellie's idea of good

publicity. Her idea of advertising was a discreet calling card: CAMP HOTEL—Friends Easily Made. "When you are running a house," she once told a judge, "you don't tell everybody what you do for a living. You try to do it the best way you can and use your own ideas and it is just pure luck."

Nellie's luck was good. Shortly after she began looking for a new location, the Japanese evacuation made the Outlook available. She bought out the Kodamas' lease, and set about remodeling it into her idea of a bordello: a quiet place with a touch of class in its appointments, away from rival establishments but with considerable pedestrian traffic nearby, and with enough rooms so that some could be used for legitimate hotel purposes, thus providing a cover for more profitable activities. She renamed the place LaSalle Hotel, which sounded toney and implied a possible French connection. She had it rewired, replumbed, and repainted— cream with dark brown trim; she put new carpeting in the halls, the three landings,

---

ABOVE: *Nellie's first brothel in Seattle was the Camp Hotel at 1929 First Avenue. It was a second-story walk-up in a frame clapboard building—typical of such establishments except that it was north of the Skid Road. (King County Assessor's Office)*

FACING PAGE: *The Japanese evacuation made the LaSalle Hotel, which basked in the glow of the Public Market sign, available for transformation into the house of Nellie's dreams. (City of Seattle)*

and the connecting stairway. She shopped at Grunbaum's for classy furniture, as she later testified during a court case:

> I had the dresser, a very large dresser and a big mirror and a chiffonier and they were massive sets, very good furniture. And I had the bed, the spring, and the mattress, and then I had beautiful chairs. They cost from $50 to $60 and $75, silk, in all the rooms, and I had rockers, stationary rockers that stand still and you can rock yourself, and I had the bookstands, floor lamps, and I had linoleum rugs, besides five or six other rugs, and I had cigarette stands.

The LaSalle was almost too successful. One afternoon shortly after it opened, a few girls of obvious charm met the boats coming in for shore leave and distributed calling cards. That evening there were what seemed to the shore patrol a thousand gobs lined up outside the LaSalle, waiting for space in its fifty-seven berths. The military immediately put the place off limits, Mayor William Devin ordered a crackdown on prostitution, and Peaches, Creamy, and the other attractions of Nellie's place confined their ministrations to members of the home front for the duration.

After that one embarrassment, the LaSalle merged into the background of the Market, attracting little attention. On a typical day, Nellie would sleep till mid-afternoon, perhaps venture out before the shops closed to buy a pint of cream at the Fairmount Creamery at First and

were actually in search of lodging must have wondered at the elegance of her clothes in a place whose only entrance was next to a tavern called the Place Pigalle.

During quiet moments at the shop, Nellie worked on the books, which were as accurate as she could make them as far as permanent guests were concerned. They showed annual gross incomes between $20,000 and $31,000. As for the short-order customers, the I.R.S. found her accounting suspect: the books could not explain Nellie's Cadillacs, ermine, pearls, an extravagance of hats, and frequent trips to Las Vegas, Los Angeles, and New York.

Some of Nellie's travel was for her health. She suffered from glaucoma that became increasingly painful around 1945 and led to her decision to withdraw from active management. In 1947, she sold a half-interest in the business to her nephew, Max Elias, and went to Hot Springs, Arkansas, for a protracted rest. When Mayor Devin won re-election in 1948 on a renewed promise to clean up the town, she wrote Max a reassuring letter:

> Now about the election—well it's too bad, and then again who cares? I have been at the same deal, with tougher ones and mean ones and I am still in the same place doing the same, and I took my ups and downs, worse than at present and came out on top so it doesn't matter to me who gets in, I will always find my own outs, and go

Stewart, dine in her three-room suite, and just before eight in the evening, check the linen cupboards to be sure there was an ample supply of towels and sheets. She'd check herself in the mirror—hair in place, four-screen satin blouse smooth, pearl necklace hanging with the biggest pearls down—then relieve Gladys, who presided over the reception desk during the day.

Nellie was usually on hand through the peak hours, midnight until two, and sometimes stayed on duty until 8 A.M. She was a small, birdlike woman with friendly eyes and a warm laugh. Naive guests who

---

ABOVE: *On the stairway down toward Western Avenue, the Place Pigalle offered other comforts for the lonely. (Photo by Mary Randlett)*

FACING PAGE: *The tavern's ambience included candle-in-a-bottle illumination, a table with a view, and a clientele given to wearing hats at the bar. (Sketch by Laurie Olin)*

as I am. I have paid more with better ones and got less—so going as I am I will still eat and some. I have known thieves and robbers—hold-up men in that same office—so with Devin in again is just as good, and am just as satisfied—so what?

Max turned out to be an unsatisfactory madam, so Nellie returned to Seattle and resumed management of the LaSalle. After an argument with his aunt, Max filed suit for his share of the profits between June 1, 1947 and April 25, 1948, demanding an accounting for all receipts and expenditures during that period. Rather than make her accounts a matter of public record, Nellie settled out of court.

In April 1949, a major earthquake struck Seattle. The LaSalle swayed and groaned on its perch above Western Avenue. The temblor struck at midday, so it is unlikely any patrons were rewarded with unanticipated excitement. Such was not the case in Carly Westcott's barbershop in the basement of the Public Market Building. It was Carly's practice to put a broad restraining strap across a

FROM TOP TO BOTTOM: *The flower shop would wither as blight was removed. Manning's had become Lowell's, but the view was the same. The vegetables could be kept fresh, but could the stalls survive?* (Seattle Times)

man's chest after he had been tilted back in the chair for a shave. A customer was reclining, partly shaved, when the building began to sway. Carly bolted. The lights went out as she raced up the ramp, but she ran for daylight and burst out onto Pike Place, surprised that people scattered as she approached. Then she realized she was still carrying the open razor. It was some time before she worked her way back to the shop and unbuckled the man in the chair. He declined the rest of the shave.

No one was hurt at the LaSalle, but Nellie's confidence was shaken. The ground wasn't firm, family members were undependable, and the Market wasn't doing the business that characterized the wartime years. She decided it was time for a change and let it be known her lease on the hotel was available.

George and Sodeko Ikeda, a Japanese American couple that had returned from the evacuation, were among those interested. Accompanied by a real estate agent, they paid three visits to the LaSalle, checking the heating plant, examining the foundation, and going over the registration cards with Gladys Westbrooke, the desk clerk. The cards indicated there were thirty-four permanent residents.

The Ikedas wanted to talk to Nellie about the business. After being told several times she was too ill to see them, they were granted an audience in Nellie's chamber, Room 219, on October 9, 1951. She sat in a platform rocker, looking small amidst piles of hats that reached almost to the ceiling. Their talk was all business. Nellie said the recent monthly receipts ranged from $1,900 to $2,300; Ikeda said that seemed too high. Nellie explained that she did a big overnight trade with merchant seamen and her advertising program had made the LaSalle well known in distant places. At one point, Nellie had to look for a key to open a cupboard where records were kept. Ikeda recalled the scene later: "So she was looking, pulling out the drawers and trying to find the key, but she couldn't find the key . . . I saw a lot of money in every drawer she pulled out. . . . She had a vanity and dresser. She pulled out the lampstand drawers too. And in every drawer she pulled out she had a lot of cash. Some was lying flat, some was stacked up."

The Ikedas bought the business. Nellie moved out, hats, money, and all, leaving the Market, but not the profession. She leased the St. Clair half a mile away and, in the lumber town of Aberdeen, leased the building of a defunct bank, which at least solved her problem of where to stash loose cash.

As for the Ikedas, they found the LaSalle not as represented. There were only twelve regular guests, not thirty-four. (Nellie may have counted rooms occupied by her business manager, Antoinette Sodini, her porter-chauffeur, Peaches, Creamy, and their sisters.) Nor was the transient trade drawn by the wonders of the view from the bay windows. George Ikeda recalled his first day at the desk, October 18, 1951:

About seventeen or eighteen men came in during the daytime while I was at the desk. They came up to ask about the girls and I told them it was under new hand and I don't have any girls, and he said, "You don't have to be scared, I am seaman." And he pulled out his identification cards. But I said, "I am sorry. I don't have any girls here, see?" And they said, "Where is Mrs. Curtis; where is Gladys?" And I told them, "I don't know, they left no forwarding address; I don't know how to locate them."

Bob, the Ikeda's son, was a pre-law student at the University of Washington and clerked weekends. He had the same experience. From thirty to fifty men would check in and ask for girls. Told there were none, some would smile, nod, take a room and wait. After a while they'd be back at the desk.

"OK Mac, where are the girls?"

"I told you. No girls."

"No girls? OK—but it's a hell of a way to run a whorehouse!"

Finally, acting on advice from their attorneys, the Ikedas had a sign posted at 83 Pike Street, next to the tavern: No Girls. Business was very bad, so they sued, claiming fraud. They had paid $17,500 for the lease, furniture, equipment, hotel license, and good will. Of good will they had none. They won in King County Superior Court, but Nellie appealed. The State Supreme Court also ruled for the Ikedas: $7,500 plus interest.

Nellie's day at the Market was over.

Chapter 9 | DREAMS AND NIGHTMARES

After the war, the Market had two big problems: not enough farmers and not enough customers.

Few of those who remained on the soil during the war were of a mind to hawk their produce from stalls. The military bought in huge quantities from wholesalers, who in turn contracted for all a farmer could deliver. Efficiency lay not in truck farming but in growing a single crop and selling it to one buyer. The Farm Security Administration made it easy to borrow money for land and equipment. The Immigration Service made it easy to bring in stoop labor from Mexico for seasonal work. These forces led to larger farms but fewer full-time farmers.

When the war ended and the Japanese returned, many were unable to get their former land back. The Issei who did go back to the land encountered a problem familiar to immigrant farmers of other nationalities: their children did not look to the soil for a livelihood. Mrs. Mike Iannioelle of Des Moines, who had been selling produce from her six-acre garden in the Market for thirty years, summed it up: "Business is not good. Nothing like before the war. Everybody buys from supermarkets. The young people, they don't want to work on the land. I have five children. They all leave home for business and white collars and clean hands. Why should they break their back on the farm?"

Even those willing to do the work had to compete with highways and industries for suitable land. New roads encouraged the flight to the suburbs and brought more developers into the competition for acreage. Rezoning to industrial or commercial status raised taxes on farms to the point where some who wanted to keep on raising crops were forced to sell just to pay back taxes.

Farmer-vendor licenses declined ninety percent in a quarter century. The Market Master issued 515 licenses in 1939. In 1949 there were only 53.

Fewer customers came to the Market. The spread of supermarkets, the advent of frozen foods, and the long-distance trucking of fresh vegetables in refrigerated trucks made it possible to get quality produce within a few blocks of most homes. Overall decline in public transportation and changes in routing made First Avenue and Pike Street less important as an exchange point. Construction of the Alaskan Way Viaduct in 1953 forced the removal of the pedestrian bridge that had linked the Market to the waterfront. First Avenue in the Market Area was turning itself from a workingman's mall into a honky-tonk

FACING PAGE: *Somebody always wanted to throw the Market to the Future. In 1950, Harlan Edwards proposed a seven-story garage with a luxury restaurant, specialty shops, a department store, and even some space for selling green goods. (City of Seattle)*

BELOW: *When the city council in 1947 forbade singing by vendors, Morris Levy raised his voice in protest while Sue Manzo tried to shush him. "Here is spring and the gag rule keeps men shut up like a mummy. . . . A frog can flush his face and sing in the springtime. But Morris Levy, can he sing in the Market? No! For him it is shut up and sell the lettuce quiet."* (Seattle Times)

fewer workingmen, more seniors. You might see an old man with a cane helping himself along a railing, another with two canes taking minutes to cross Pike Place, a bent woman in black dress, black turban, and long beige stockings crabbing into a doorway, all three carrying shopping bags, each picking out just enough food for the day. They had grown old with the Market, and the aging buildings were friends.

strip featuring porno peep shows and other diversions for the unimaginative. Pike Place was becoming not a hub but an island.

Facilities were deteriorating. The Sanitary Market had been rebuilt immediately after the 1941 fire, but the war years saw little new construction and much deferred maintenance. Paint was peeling from the walls of most of the buildings, marquees hung unevenly from rusting chains, floors sloped, wooden buildings leaned against their masonry neighbors.

The Market's clientele had aged, too. The pace was slower; there were few days of crowded aisles, and shopping in the off-hours was leisurely and conversational. Nearby hotels and apartments housed

The Market was their club. But there were those who found the deterioration deplorable.

In February 1950 the *Post-Intelligencer* ran a ten-part series on possible solutions to Seattle's traffic problems. In the final article, Harlan Edwards, a Seattle civil and structural engineer then serving on the city planning commission, proposed to alleviate the downtown-parking problem by demolishing the Market and replacing it with a seven-story garage. The garage roof, level with First Avenue, was to be a park, landscaped with grass, rhododendrons, firs, and ferns. Adjoining or beneath the park, Edwards proposed a "first-class restaurant, shops dealing in

curious and distinctive Pacific Northwest projects, and possible department store concessions." As for the Market itself, the garage would have space for "public market stalls" and a central checkroom where "merchants could deliver parcels purchased during the day." To make space for the new facility, all buildings between First Avenue and Western Avenue from Stewart to Pike would be torn down. The destruction of the old Market would be a civic benefit, removing "a blighted area which is now a fire and life hazard to the people using it."

Mark Tobey was appalled. He was fifty-nine-years old, a most apolitical man, solitary by nature, no organizer of crusades, but he hated impersonal architecture: "Landmarks with human dimensions are being torn down to be replaced by structures that appear never to have been touched by human hands. There seems a talent today for picking the most beautiful and personal places to destroy—what might be called an aesthetic destructive sense." And he feared the automobile: "The sense of present-day speed is also impersonal. There is no doubt that we worship the Queen of Death, the automobile." So he fired off a letter to the editor:

What do we want? A world of impersonal modernism, a world of automobiles? I've studied and painted the Paris stalls, the markets of London, Mexico, and China and none is as interesting as ours. If color and atmosphere can't be found here, people are going to spend money to find it.

Tobey's opposition was not enough by itself to kill the project (he was not yet famous in his adopted town), but his statement set the tone for later defenses of the Market.

Edwards's plan did not say how construction was to be financed. The terms of Joe Desimone's will made it all but impossible for his heirs to sell the buildings, and they had neither the inclination nor the money to carry out the project. So Edwards's gargantuan garage came no closer to reality than a handsome sketch of what it might look like. When his wife, Myrtle, was elected to the city council in 1956, she kept his plan in her office but was unable to muster support for it.

FACING PAGE, TOP: *A way of life was at stake. C. L. Primero of Kent wanted to keep his stall and did.* (Seattle Times)

FACING PAGE, BOTTOM: *The roof of Harlan Edwards's plan, extending from First Avenue, would be landscaped. (City of Seattle)*

RIGHT: *A mood of uncertainty descended upon the Market. "There seems a talent today for picking the most beautiful and personal places to destroy," thundered Mark Tobey. (University of Washington Libraries, Special Collections, photo by Mary Randlett, June 1965, MPH 317)*

The Market was spared the wrecking ball but not the effects of time. Farmers and merchants became concerned about continuing decay. In July 1956, they organized the Pike Place Farmers' Market Association to try to reverse the unfavorable trends. "We don't plan to make any sweeping changes right away," said Alvin Block, first president of the Association, in announcing its formation. "Right now, we are planning to build new business on the color and tradition that already exist in the Market. An extensive promotion campaign will be launched soon." The Association erected a sign forty feet high declaring the Market to be "SEATTLE'S BAZAAR INTERNATIONAL," ran joint advertisements in the papers, and gave cookies, doughnuts, and coffee to

---

ABOVE: *With the Market showing signs of decline, merchants organized to run advertisements, invent slogans, and host Welcome to Downtown weeks. There were more hosts (Mrs. Helen Yokoyama, Alvin Block, Mrs. Mildred Warton, and John Schonig) than customers.* (Seattle Times)

FACING PAGE: *Meanwhile Vic Steinbrueck, who helped design the Space Needle, had begun making Market sketches. (University of Washington Libraries, Special Collections, photo by Mary Randlett, Mary Randlett Collection)*

visitors during Welcome to Downtown Week. Such medicine was not strong enough.

The city's ten-year lease of arcade space for the farmers' stalls came up for renewal in 1957. Costs of maintaining the stalls had more than doubled during the decade, while revenue from license fees declined. The council seriously considered withdrawing from sponsorship of the Market it had created in 1907. Richard Desimone, representing both the Pike Place Public Market, Inc. and the Fairley Corporation, which also leased some space to the city at Pike Place, agreed to relieve the city of responsibility for major repairs in the stall area. By a six-to-three vote, the council renewed the lease, but it seemed clear changes would have to be made if the Market was not to wither or be sacrificed to profit masquerading as progress.

A year later, Mark Tobey returned to Seattle after winning first prize for international painting in the 1958 Venice Biennale, and the city council passed a resolution of civic appreciation. Tobey used the occasion of the ceremony to remind the city officials of the uniqueness and charm of his favorite institution: "If anything should happen to the Market, I feel I would want to leave Seattle." It was not to be his last word on the subject.

For some time, Seattle had seemed adrift. A caretaker city government ministered to the needs of a myopic business community that did not know what it wanted. In 1958, downtown leaders formed the Central Association of Seattle to decide what was best for the city and to get it done. Working with the City Planning Commission, they set up an agenda that centered on a Downtown Plan for 1985. While the study was being made, the Municipal Market Building on Western was destroyed by fire.

From the perspective of the business establishment and the city planners, the Pike Place Market was what Harlan Edwards called it in 1950—a blighted area—and they feared the blight was contagious. Even if the Market could be cured, its continued existence would prevent high-rise construction on view property, thus denying the city a growth in tax base and a lot of people a lot of profit.

In 1963, when the public was shown the Central Association's proposed solution to downtown malaise, lovers of the traditional Market received their traditional shock. The new vision, like the earlier plans of Doc Brown and Harlan Edwards, began with a bulldozer. This time 12.5 acres, everything from Union to Lenora, First Avenue to Western, would be leveled. This would create space for a terraced garage holding 3,000 cars (up 50 percent since 1950), a downtown park, a new hotel with magnificent view (old-timers recalled that a previous improvement, the Denny regrade, had removed the Washington Hotel, which afforded an even better view), and sites for several high-rise office buildings. A new Market could be fitted into the park, and it might become, in the words of Central Association President Ben Ehrlichman, "a visitor and tourist attraction quite equal to the Los Angeles Farmers' Market."

Victor Steinbrueck, a University of Washington professor of architecture who had helped design the Space Needle, was the first to be heard in opposition. Steinbrueck had grown up in Seattle. When young, he assumed that "such a Market was an essential part of every city, like a post office or a railroad station." He had been amazed on his first visit to Los Angeles in 1935 to find no equivalent of Pike Place. The artificially created Farmers' Market that later appeared in Los Angeles and which Ben Ehrlichman cited as something the Central Association plan might bestow on Seattle, Steinbrueck thought "a horrible example of what could happen."

Speaking at a hearing on September 13, 1963, Steinbrueck told the City Planning Commission: "It would be a major catastrophe if the plan was executed. It is an unimaginative little plan. It is not a

great plan worthy of Seattle's future nor appropriate to the city's unique setting." He kept up the sniping. "It's not termites from within that will make the Market collapse," he warned, "it's termites from without." As for building a Los Angeles-style plastic market, it would be like "replacing grandmother with a chorus girl."

But the Establishment steamroller was not to be diverted with rhetoric. Plans to implement Downtown 1985 were developed. The Central Association was anticipating a massive infusion of federal urban renewal funds to help remove blight. (Government involvement would also allow condemnation of land needed for the project, thus bypassing the clause of Joe Desimone's will that forbade sale of the Market buildings.) The city council had previously created a citizen's committee, Seattle Urban Renewal Enterprise (SURE), to give advice on urban renewal matters. Most of its members had backgrounds in real estate and land development and were anxious to see the Downtown Plan advanced. A joint committee with members from SURE, the Seattle Real Estate Board, and the Central Association was appointed to review downtown blight and suggest a special urban renewal project.

By August 1964, the committee had settled on a specific plan for the 12.5 acres. "Seattle people have been asking for some bold step which will preserve the Go-ahead spirit of the 1962 World Fair and consolidate its gains," it declared. "We believe this is it." The plan was formally submitted to Mayor Dorm Braman on September 1, with the prediction that tax returns from the area would increase a thousand percent because of redevelopment. In January, the Mayor and city council directed that city urban renewal officials prepare an application to the Department of Housing and Urban Development for funds to cover surveys and planning for what they styled the Pike Plaza Redevelopment Project.

Wing Luke, the city councilman most sympathetic to the Market, urged that opponents organize to bring pressure for Market preservation. Later in the summer, Luke's friend, Robert Ashley, an attorney, helped arrange a champagne breakfast for some sixty sympathizers on the balcony of Lowell's. Those assembled were short on political clout but long on pithy and poetic statements of what the Market meant to them. Architect Fred Bassetti had to miss the meeting, but sent a statement describing the Market as "an honest place in a phony time." Its roughness reminded him "of Seattle's beginnings, its lusty past, the vitality that gave it national notice long ago. . . . It needs the hammer and paint brush, not the black ball of destruction."

Also read was the introduction to Mark Tobey's *The World of a Market* that the University of Washington Press was about to publish. It began with the statement:

> The sketches in this book show my feelings for the Seattle Market perhaps much better than anything I can say about it. And yet there seems to be a need to speak, today, when drastic changes are going on all around us. Our homes are in the path of freeways; old landmarks, many of a rare beauty, are sacrificed to the urge to get somewhere in a hurry; and when it is all over Progress reigns, queen of hollow streets shadowed by monumental towers left behind by giants to whom the intimacy of living is of no importance. The moon is still far away, but there are forces close by which are ready, with high-sounding words, to dump you out of bed and tear from your sight the colors of joy.

figures appear and disappear, and then the Market is quiet, awaiting another day.

That meeting led to general agreement that the Market would have to be preserved. No new structure could have the old one's warmth and naturalness, the lived-in quality, the surprises caused by architectural decisions made years ago to meet problems long forgotten. No matter how hard the developers tried, they'd only construct another mall, sterile as a Hollywood conception of the future.

Out of the get-together on the balcony at Lowell's grew the organization known as Friends of the Market. Vic Steinbrueck and Robert Ashley served as co-chairmen. It was agreed that the Friends' first task would be to remind the town of what it stood to lose if the black ball of destruction were let loose at Pike Place.

The operation was hardly high-powered. The Friends opened an office at the Market. They sold Tobey's *World of a Market*, Steinbrueck's *Seattle Cityscape* and later his delightful *Market Sketchbook*, shopping bags, two Market recipe books, and Market sunflower buttons. They guided

And now this unique Market is in danger of being modernized like so much processed cheese.

Tobey ended sadly:

The years dissolve, and I return to visit the Market. A few old friends remain—the brothers of the fish stall, but the interesting sign above their heads has been stolen. The chairs that ascended the incline directly below them, upon which tired shoppers used to rest, have been torn out. But the main part of the Market is still active, still varied, exciting, and terribly important in the welter of over-industrialization. There is the same magic as night approaches: the sounds fade; there is an extra rustle everywhere; prices drop; the garbage pickers come bending and sorting; the cars leave the street which reflects the dying sun. The windows are all that remain of light as the sun sets over the Olympics. A few isolated

Above: *Under the lighting designed by Frank Goodwin, between the neon advertising Maurie's chicken (barbequed or fresh) and the neo-Victorian arches of the Bank of Commerce, a new organization hung up its shingle: Friends of the Market. (University of Washington Libraries, Special Collections, photo by Mary Randlett, March 1967, MPH 348)*

When Mayor Braman named a Pike Place Advisory Committee, its chairman, Donald Voorhees, an attorney who had previously been chairman of SURE, made conciliatory sounds about keeping the Market "pretty much as it is" if possible. The Advisory Committee then named architects Paul Kirk and John Morse, whom no one considered insensitive to environmental concerns, as the team to draw plans for several approaches to Pike Plaza development.

While the designs were being prepared, there was a pause in the skirmishing, but not in behind the scenes maneuvering. A group of local entrepreneurs incorporated themselves as the Central Park Plaza Corporation, elected William Ferguson (an attorney who had served as chairman of the Central Association's Pike Place committee) as their president, and began buying land in and near the proposed development area. They took the position that they were only responding to Mayor Braman's expressed hope that private enterprise would assure that the property to be urban developed would be fully utilized and that the money for development was in sight. Everyone denied that Central Park Plaza was sure to get the assignment if development was approved, but no one else bothered to enter the lists.

The lull ended in March 1968 when the city, which had acquired the old Washington National Guard Armory a block from the Market, tore it down. Citizens who protested, including architects Laurie Olin and Fred Bassetti, were told that the design team's plans, which had not been made public, called for running a road through the armory site.

Against this background of wrecking ball improvement, the design team revealed its five alternative proposals. A model of the one favored by the design

walking tours of the Market. Members appeared before the city council and planning commission, service organizations, and church groups. In cooperation with the Seattle Junior Chamber of Commerce, they planted trees, shrubs, and flowers on an open hillside near the Market. They wrote letters to editors, cultivated reporters, and solicited articles from national writers concerned about the environment and historic preservation. Delighted with the warmth of their reception, they began to feel they were not just throwing snowballs at the tank column. On the other hand, Wing Luke's death in a plane crash deprived the Friends of their council ally.

The city and the Central Association began to talk compromise. Paul Seibert of the business group declared that retention of the "general heart of the market" was both desirable and possible.

team and drawings of the others were exhibited at the Market. The favored design (first called Proposal 21, later modified and known as Scheme 23) proposed leaving the L-shaped Main Market Building in place and giving it a new copper roof. Everything else would have to go to make room for parking for 4,000 cars, a 32-story apartment building for elderly and low-income tenants, a

FACING PAGE: *Everyone had designs on, or for, the Market. Professor Steinbrueck, getting folksier by the moment, examines the winner in a Market bag competition.* (Seattle Times)

TOP: *A model of the urban renewal proposal.* (City of Seattle)

BOTTOM: *A pro-urban renewal sketch emphasizing the parklike aspects of what would be left of the traditional Market.* (Sketch by Peter Staten)

quartet of 28-story apartments for the affluent, 300,000 feet of office space, and a hockey arena.

The immediate response from the Friends was friendly. Vic Steinbrueck was spending a sabbatical year in England. Robert Ashley, now soloing as chairman, was pleased that at least the central building was saved, and said so. But second thoughts were far from positive.

Fred Bassetti, who had been Morse's partner, complained that the Morse-Kirk plan left the Market a refugee at home, "isolated and adrift in an alien environment." Steinbueck wrote from London that under the proposed plan, the Market could neither "retain its character nor continue to serve low-income shoppers nor provide space for low-income merchants." Late in the month, the Friends took the official position that the plan "could have a brutal and overpowering effect upon the intricate social and merchandising conditions in the Market and that all possible effort must be made to provide a sympathetic environment in the area surrounding the market."

Mayor Braman, addressing the Rotary Club on April 14, 1968, denounced the denouncers as "nitpickers." He described the Market as "a decadent, somnolent fire-trap." As for the argument that urban renewal was "urban removal" and forced the evacuation of people from their homes, he saw no reason why they should be left in the middle of such a choice area. The goal of the project was "to bring the money and brainpower of the best people back into Seattle."

Kirk and Morse were more sympathetic to the Friends. During the six months before the council finally authorized forwarding the plan to HUD for its reaction and comments, they made numerous changes. The Corner Market and Economy Market would be retained, the proposed new copper roof on the Main Market Building was eliminated, and it was the stated purpose of the design to preserve the look of the original wherever possible. The thirty-story high-rise for low-income folk became a constellation of six smaller buildings of various heights. The LaSalle Hotel (without any Nellie Curtis amenities) would be restored for low-income housing, as would the Leland Hotel across Pike Street.

The Friends acknowledged the changes as a manifestation of good intention, but were not satisfied. They refused to believe it would be possible for the Market, which they were coming to view more in ecological than architectural terms, to survive amid the glare and shadow of all that glass and steel and concrete. They saw their Market as a unique organism that had evolved out of a combination of local circumstances that could never be repeated. The proposed Plaza would be an artificial thing created by mating a bureaucrat's desire to expand the tax base with an entrepreneur's lust for profit.

It took HUD six months to review the plan, determine that it conformed to the guidelines, stamp it acceptable, and send it back to Seattle for final approval by the council, which was needed before HUD would consider the city's application for funds. The Friends spent the intervening time circulating a petition asking the city council to endorse "conservation and sympathetic rehabilitation" of the Market rather than reconstruction. They aimed at getting 47,781 signatures, which someone had estimated would make a roll reaching from the Market to the Municipal Building. They obtained more than

FACING PAGE: *Mike Marush ponders the fate of the Athenian, long a favorite with shoppers and workers. Nearly any need could be met at the Market—flowers, funerals, false teeth. The Pike Place Fish Market's best advertisements were its trays of shining fish. (University of Washington Libraries, Special Collections, photos by Mary Randlett, March 1967, Mary Randlett Collection)*

ABOVE: *The old-timers in the stalls wondered how long they would be putting their fresh radishes and onions and squash on the counters of the farmers' arcade. (University of Washington Libraries, Special Collections, photos by Mary Randlett, April 1965, Mary Randlett Collection)*

53,000. Steinbrueck says of the petition: "We requested retention of the Market generally, its structures, the farmers, the small business, and the low-income residents. Since this was not an official initiative petition, it was politely accepted and unanimously ignored by the City Council."

The hearings on Scheme 23, as the modified plan was now called, opened on March 19 and closed April 25. Twelve sessions were held on ten separate days, thirty-three hours and thirty minutes of testimony were recorded, and eighty documents were submitted. Phalanges of partisans—pro-renewal people

---

ABOVE: *Architect Laurie Olin drew this sketch during the city council hearings on the urban renewal proposal. He sought to show how the neighboring high-rises would change the Market atmosphere. (Courtesy of Laurie Olin)*

mostly in business suits and pro-Market forces a motley carrying banners (Beware of Plastic Markets) and daffodils—applauded their champions. Mayor Braman compared the protesters to those people who had derided the Century 21 World Fair, then claimed credit for its success. Vic Steinbrueck, back from England, declared "The Big Lie, the quarter-truth, is that the market is being saved." Laurie Olin, an architect and member of the Friends of the Market, recalls the hearings, which he sketched:

> I do have some clear recollections of some of the events, the grueling tedium of having to wreck our days and lives to go up to city hall to sit in that room, full of tension and animosity, to fight for something that the government should have been the defender/caretaker of—finally it became a war of attrition on their part—trying to wear us all down, drag it out and hope that we would become fatalistic, tired, or divided. As it turned out the planners and governmental people, their powerful friends in the financial community drew us together as we never could quite do on our own. On our part it became more than a cause, but a case of community education and interaction. . . . Here the issue finally came down to one of social thought, not architecture. It was urban souls who believed in diversity and felt that the haves must face up to their brothers, the have nots: that whatever was wrong with downtown Seattle, it was not the public market and its denizens, but rather the grim vision and lives of the more affluent who neither lived in nor liked the city. In my own little presentation—which was to try and once and for all show

them that the market was not a series of buildings but a community—I described the market in terms of ecology (both plant and human ecology) and showed diagrams of what different people saw as "The Market," from Mark Tobey, through Urban Renewal, Friends of the Market, an economic consultant to the City, etc. It was hard, short, partially scholarly, and certainly impassioned (I choked and gasped for air a few times, my heart was beating so, for I still am, like many people, intimidated by authority). To my amazement, the city council all applauded when I finished—something they certainly hadn't done before. My wife sitting in the audience overheard two elderly ladies behind her say "despite all that hair you can tell, he's had a fine education." I may have looked a bit freaky to them, for this was the year after the Chicago riots at the Democratic Convention—Kent State was yet to come, but the polarization of life styles, ideas, and solutions to the mounting problems was a large and awesome fact. The battle over the market was in some ways part of that pervasive intellectual crisis in American society.

Not a vote was changed. The council voted unanimously to adopt the plan, though they did suggest the developer explore the idea of retaining through rehabilitation the Butterworth Building, Alaska Trade Building, and the Fairmount Hotel, and of reducing the height of the hotel building. On August 11, 1969, the council voted to request $2 million in neighborhood development funds for the first year of urban renewal.

At this point, the Friends received help from an unexpected source. The

Nixon administration issued new guidelines for Neighborhood Development Projects. The Pike Plaza project would have to be submitted under a different category, and there would be a delay of at least eighteen months before it could be processed. The times they were a-changin', as a protest song of the day phrased it—and the changes worked to the advantage of the Friends. Nixon's failure to find a quick way out of the Vietnam War and the enormous layoffs at Boeing created an atmosphere of suspicion about all official pronounce-

ments. Even Establishment supporters of the Park Plaza developed sudden doubts about the need for all that cubed space, and about the availability of money to finance cubing.

At this point, Steinbrueck made a surprise attack and opened a new front. The National Historic Preservation Act of 1966 established a State Advisory Council on Historic Preservation and a National Register of Historic Places. Steinbrueck and Laurie Olin presented the State Advisory Council with documents making the case for creation of a seventeen-acre Pike Place Market Historic District. The council, after quiet deliberation, accepted the proposal. The historic district embraced more than two-thirds of the land involved in the Pike Plaza renewal proposal. The catch was the Historic Sites Act mandated that no public money could be spent inside a registered Historic Place, without prior approval by the Advisory Council on Historic Preservation. Steinbrueck's coup seemed sure to slow and possibly to kill the project.

Establishment forces counterattacked. They persuaded Charles Odegaard, chairman of the State Advisory Council, to call a special meeting to reconsider their action. After a tour of the project area in company with city officials and a two-week period of pondering, the Advisory Council reduced the Historic Site from 17 acres to 1.7. What was left included the Economy Market, Corner Market, and Pike Place Market from Pike to Pine. The Council asked the city to honor a "historical buffer" of about a block and a half around the buildings designated in the National Register.

The Friends, joined by the Washington Environmental Council and three merchants with businesses in the Market, filed suit, claiming Odegaard had exceeded his authority in reopening the question and asking restoration of the original seventeen acres to the National Register. The city filed a motion for dismissal. It was denied, but the case never came to trial.

The final campaign in the seven-year battle began in May 1971. HUD offices in Washington announced on May 15 that the $10,600,000 Pike Plaza project was approved. Federal funds would be available. The next day, the Friends revealed their last weapon: an initiative campaign to establish a seven-acre Historical District.

The initiative and petitions for its submission to the voters had already been drawn. It called for a district running from Virginia to a line between Pike and Union, from the middle of First to the middle of Western. Supervision of the

FACING PAGE: *Friends of the Market poster called supporters to the council for the urban renewal hearing.*

TOP TO BOTTOM: *Laurie Olin, besides testifying, sketched council members "Sitting in Judgment against the Market." Sam Smith and Tim Hill, Ted Best and J. Paul Alexander, and Mitchell and Charles Carroll.*

area was to be in the hands of a Market Historical Commission which would have as its function "the preservation, restoration and improvement" of the buildings and "the continuance of uses deemed to have architectural, cultural, economic and historical value." The membership of the committee would be drawn from designated groups, a preponderance of which shared the Friends' values.

To get the initiative on the ballot, the Friends would need 15,560 legal signatures from registered Seattle voters. They aimed at collecting 20,000, to allow for slippage; in three weeks they had 25,478. The city council had to put the initiative on the November ballot.

Looking back at the result of the election—Initiative No. 1 carried overwhelmingly, winning more than 60 percent of the vote and running ahead in four out of five precincts—it seems that victory for the Market had been all but certain from the moment the measure was put on the ballot. Nevertheless, the campaign was carried on with deep commitment, clawing fury, and rampant suspicion.

The Friends had more visibility than political experience. They were not organized by precinct or tied closely to any group that was, they knew little about lining up advertising time and space, and they had more volunteers than discipline. Their leadership consisted of people who

worked best on their own, and their principal strategist, Steinbrueck, was in England from May to September completing his sabbatical.

Watching the early stages of the initiative campaign from the fringe, a number of younger activists became alarmed. Many were relatively new to Seattle but experienced in various anti-Establishment campaigns (anti-freeway, anti-Vietnam, anti-Nixon). They came to regard the Friends as hopelessly artsy-fartsy, so blindly optimistic, so hung up on ecological issues that they would blow the campaign, especially when big money began to flow in the latter stages.

These Young Turks united in a new group, the Alliance for a Living Market. The key figures in its formation were Jack Bagdade, a young physician who fell in love with the Market after coming to Seattle in 1965 for his medical residency; Tim Manring, a young attorney active in the civic reform group known as Choose an Effective City Council—CHECC; Susan French, another young attorney; Jack Levy of City Fish; and Frank Miller, a member of the commune that ran the Soup and Salad Restaurant in the Market.

The Alliance recruited Al Pierce, a University of Washington graduate student in political science who had worked with the Kennedy organization, as their manager, but his Massachusetts manner proved abrasive; when he eventually resigned to return to his studies he was replaced by Harriet Sherburne. Sherburne was from Seattle but had picked up political experience during a stay in Chicago.

The Friends and the Alliance were uneasy allies, but they managed to stay in harness, held together by shared fury at the tactics of the opposition.

The city council put the Market initiative on the November general election ballot rather than the September primary to give the Pike Plaza forces time to organize. The council also approved a competing initiative, proposed by Mayor Wes Uhlman, which called for a much smaller district, one that would merely protect historic associations. State law prohibited city officials from campaigning directly against Initiative No. 1, but they leaned in technically nonpartisan ways toward solutions that would "retain the flavor" of the Market while permitting most of the area to be leveled and reassembled.

It was practical politics, not state law, which kept the Central Association from leading the fight against the Market Initiative: the campaign should not be

FACING PAGE: *Vic Steinbrueck sketches and plans. (University of Washington Libraries, Special Collections, Mary Randlett Collection)*

ABOVE: *The Friends and Alliance had most of the artists. Pro-initiative campaign buttons outnumbered the antis by six to one.*

identified with the developers. But those who would benefit most by the defeat of the initiative got together, hired a twenty-seven-year old public relations consultant named Mike MacEwan, guaranteed ample funds for a campaign (they eventually reported raising about $23,000), and on August 20 announced themselves as The Committee to Save the Market at 81 Pike Place. (It was this that led to the formation three weeks later of the Alliance for a Living Market.)

Besides easy access to money, MacEwan's group had the advantage of support from Richard Desimone (who contributed $3,000) and some of the better-known tenants in the Market, including Reid Lowell of the restaurant, and Pete De Laurenti of the grocery. Their names gave weight to the Committee's claim that it represented those truly interested in the Market, and

made plausible advertisements under headings such as "Pike Place Merchants Ask Your Support," which declared: "We've been analyzed, scrutinized and idolized by every hippie, do-gooder and dilettante who has needed a special project to earn a market merit badge. We're sick of it—vote No."

The Alliance counterattack centered on the theme that the economics of the Pike Plaza development were dubious. The Boeing boom had busted. There were plenty of apartments available in Seattle (13.2 percent vacancy), the big hotels rattled along half empty, demand for office space was down. Who was going to finance the building of all those proposed high-rises at this time? Would urban renewal clearance mean a long period of desolation before redevelopment? Where would the displaced find jobs? Would the dislocations mean that small merchants would go out of business and only those embodying Ghirardelli Square chic survive?

Such questions were given more power when CHECC led a campaign to get the Friends, the Alliance, and the Committee to reveal the sources of their financial support prior to the October 31 deadline set by the recently adopted Public Disclosure initiative. Reluctantly, the Committee to Save the Market opened its books; gleefully the Alliance and Friends opened theirs. Contributions for the latter two had come in dollops from individuals. The Committee's money had come in chunks of $1,000 to $2,500 from the likes of Sea-First, Safeco, Washington International Hotels, Central Park Plaza, and Frederick & Nelson—this despite poor Mike MacEwan's previous denials that the Committee was fronting for the downtown Establishment.

The last few days before the election saw a blizzard of claims and counter-claims, interpretations and reinterpretations of what passage of the initiative would mean to the Market. What would happen to the promised HUD funds if the initiative passed? Would federal money be lost to Seattle as city officials indicated, or could it be spent under terms controlled by provisions of the initiative?

By the time voters went to the polls, there was no doubt that nearly everybody wanted to save the Market. The question was, who could be trusted to save it? At this point the tweedy figure of Vic Steinbrueck may have been the most important symbol. He clearly loved the Market and he had been proved right on many disputed points. He couldn't have done it by himself. It probably couldn't have been done without him:

Initiative No. 1: Yes, 76,369; No, 53,264.

The voters had created a seven-acre historical district and the Market Historical Commission to oversee it. The campaign committee dissolved, but the issues persisted.

FACING PAGE: *Opposition to the Save the Market initiative stressed the theme sounded early by Mayor Dorm Braman, who described it as "a decadent, somnolent fire-trap." (Courtesy of Victor Steinbrueck)*

BELOW: *The Honor Roll—Friends of the Market autographed the wall in their campaign headquarters. (Photo by Mary Randlett)*

Chapter 10 | THE FRUITS AND THORNS OF VICTORY

The election ended the argument over whether the
Market should be saved. The voters had spoken
loud and clear. How to save it was now the question.

Many stalls were empty. There had been 600 permit
holders in the thirties; now there were 60. Unsure about
the economic future of the area, property owners (many
of them out-of-town heirs or bank trusts) had downplayed
upkeep. Paint was peeling, plumbing leaking, roofs
sagging, floors cracking, and, in many buildings, the
wiring system was both threat and puzzle. Building code
enforcement in the Market district reduced the fire
danger by closing hotels, causing resident population to

drop from 440 in 1968 to 175 in 1974. Most of those who remained were single, elderly, and male. With fewer neighbors, fewer customers, fewer tenants and decrepit buildings, the Market presented its would-be saviors with a Rubik's cube of interlocking problems. There was no shortage of officials, commissions, and committees anxious to line things up.

City officials became instant converts to the concept of preservation they had thought quixotic during the initiative campaign. James Braman, director of the city's Department of Community Development (which was responsible for urban renewal programs), showed up at the election night celebration of the Friends of the Market with his wrists wrapped in make-believe bandages stained with red paint. "The people have spoken," he said in his surrender speech. "Let's work together."

The city council moved swiftly to pass an ordinance adopting and implementing the provisions of the initiative. It established within the twenty-two-acre urban renewal area a seven-acre Market Historical District in which buildings retained for Market activities were to have "a general harmony as to style, form, color, proportion, texture, material, occupancy and use." A Market Historical Commission was created to interpret the ordinance and provide guidelines for building restoration and regulatory oversight.

The initiative mandated that the Market Historical Commission be comprised of two members from the Friends of the Market, two from the Seattle Chapter of the American Institute of Architects, two from Allied Arts of Seattle, two Market property owners, two Market merchants, and two residents of the historical district. Mayor Wes Uhlman's appointees included many figures that

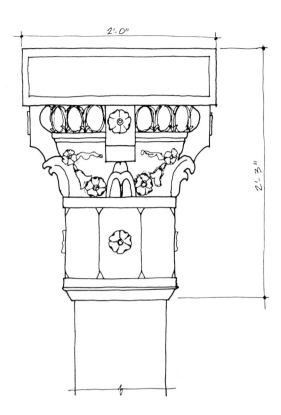

had been prominent in the fight over the initiative—most, though not all, on the winning side.

Irving Clark, Jr., attorney, ecologist, and former chairman of Allied Arts, became chairman of the Market Historical Commission. Among other members were Richard Desimone, owner of the Main Market Building; Robert Gill, owner of the Seattle Garden Center; Lee Copeland, former dean of the University of Washington College of Architecture; Dr. John Bagdade, an officer in the

---

FACING PAGE: *Without Senator Warren G. Magnuson, neither side could have won the fight over Pike Place. His leverage was needed for federal funds. Neutral during the campaign, Maggie helped the victors get money for development. (Photo by Nick Jahn)*

ABOVE: *A sketch to guide the architect in restoring columns supporting the North Arcade. (City of Seattle; sketch by Denise Etcheson)*

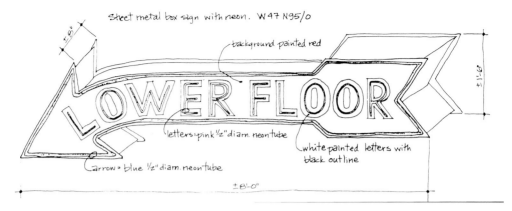

Sheet metal box sign with neon. W47 N95/0

background painted red

letters: pink ½" diam. neon tube

arrow = blue ½" diam. neon tube

white painted letters with black outline

±8'-0"

Alliance for a Living Market; Frank Miller, a member of a food commune operating in the Market, and also of the Alliance; and, inevitably, Victor Steinbrueck.

The commission, which some described as the conscience of the Market, approached its duties with religious devotion, sometimes with an inclination to theological disputation. The members gathered after business hours for their first meeting at the Barber College in the Corner Market. The site made manifest many of the physical problems they faced: the roof leaked, the temperature fluctuated, the floor groaned, and rats were numerous and bold enough to get individual nicknames. Yet the mood at the meetings reflected exhilaration. "This was the Prize," one recalled. "There we were, the veterans of the battle, saying, 'Here's our conception. This is the Market of our vision.'

First they drafted guidelines, stringent and conservative. The commission agreed that the citizens of Seattle wanted them "to maintain and perpetuate the character of the Market, responding to the changing needs of the community and, thus, retaining certain elements while absorbing new ones." With that affirmed, the commission agreed that, in evaluating applications for use or development, it would always consider: "1. The Market is a place for the farmer

to sell his produce. 2. The Market is a place for the sale of every kind of food product. 3. The Market is a place where citizens in the low- and moderate-income groups can find food, goods and services, and residences. 4. The Market is and will always be a place with the flavor of a widely varied shopping area."

Within that framework, the commission set out to encourage seventeen specific types of activity, including person-to-person sales; those offering hard-to-find goods, whether seasonal, ethnic, or for any other reason not readily available in the Seattle area; those involving light manufacturing by processes which were themselves

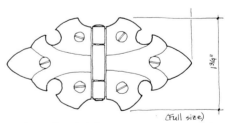

(Full size)

stamped metal hinge on Flower Row windows. Painted light green—same as window frames.

CLOCKWISE, FROM THE TOP: *Every effort was made to preserve the ambience of the Market as it was before restoration. The familiar neon sign (City of Seattle); Friends and chickens (sketch by Victor Steinbrueck); the City Fish sign on roof of North Arcade (sketch by Denise Etcheson); metal hinge on Flower Row windows (sketch by Denise Etcheson).*

Flat, painted sign

Neon tube sign on metal box

ings must harmonize in material, scale, and form with surrounding structures. Buildings and facades should be of brick, stone, or concrete, preferably unpainted, but with approved surface treatment. Facades should have a greater proportion of voids than solids at pedestrian level. Commission approval as well as a building permit would be required before work could start on razing, remodeling, or building from scratch. "The babble of sounds which characterizes the Market is an important part of the Market. Public, electronic amplification of sound is not permitted except under special circumstances."

visible and interesting; those catering particularly to the pedestrian, or offering goods for sale in a natural state as distinguished from prepackaged; those bringing together people of all backgrounds, enriching the quality of life, or relating to historical Market uses or activities.

Concerning new structures or building changes, the commission was restrictive and specific, spelling out a list of dos and don'ts calculated to "maintain the character of the Market." New build-

The commission itself sat in judgment on all proposed changes, but when it came to reviewing such questions as tenant mix, merchandising methods, or the desirability of a certain color paint, commission meetings became adversary proceedings. Decisions could be appealed to the city council, and some were—usually to no avail.

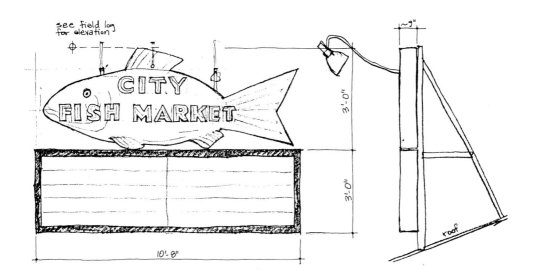

see field log for elevation

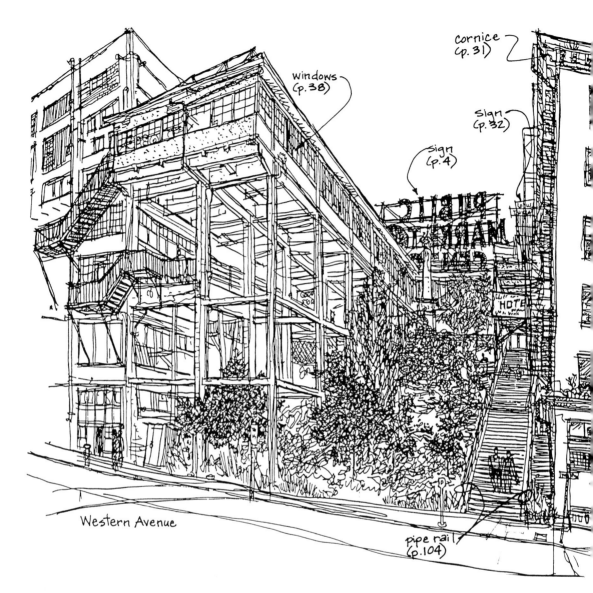

Could the trim on the Corner Market Building be French blue? The commission studied the proposed trim under three lighting conditions—morning, noon, and evening—then turned down the architect's recommendation. Could the owner of the Brasserie Pittsbourg, a French restaurant in Pioneer Square, open a restaurant in the Market? Yes—but the menu must be significantly different so as not to make it a chain. (Some old-timers noted wryly that the commission and its staff were performing the functions previously handled by the Desimones, father and son, with informal arbitrariness.)

The guidelines for the seven-acre historical district had to fit into the pattern for the twenty-two acre urban renewal district. For, in spite of the predictions by opponents of the Market initiative that its passage would kill the renewal project, it remained very much alive. Once the election was over, the city administration fought to save federal funds by dovetailing plans for the urban renewal district

ABOVE: *A Vic Steinbrueck sketch of how he hoped the stairs from Western Avenue would look. He didn't win all his battles. (City of Seattle)*

with the restrictions demanded by an historic district.

James Mason, a city planner who had previously put together a waterfront plan, was appointed Pike Project Manager. Harriet Sherburne, a key figure in the Alliance for a Living Market, served as assistant manager, then became project manager, a post she held through most of the reconstruction period. "We were making an absolute leap of faith," Sherburne declared later. "It was unprecedented to have federal urban renewal funds used in an historic district. We were trying to save a function—marketing—and nobody had ever done that."

The city staff began by documenting the Market area, writing an Historical Preservation Plan, and getting the seven acres placed on the National Register of Historic Places. This meant that before any federal money was spent on a building, there would first have to be approval from the National Advisory Council on Historic Preservation in Washington, D.C.

When Attorney Jerry Thonn of the Friends of the Market and Victor Steinbrueck were drafting the Market initiative, they included a phrase directing the proposed Market Historical Commission to develop plans for "the acquisition and perpetuation of the Pike Place Market and of market activities through either public ownership or other means." The commission appointed a subcommittee (composed of Jean Falls, a Friend of the Market and activist in Allied Arts; Randy Lee, manager of Puget Consumers Co-op; and three former members of the Alliance for a Living Market—Tim Manring, Jack Bagdade, and Frank Miller) to pursue the idea of creating a public corporation. The group met weekly, at 7 A.M., in the offices of Yale Lewis, an attorney familiar with public corporations. Out of these sessions grew

the idea of a development authority for the urban renewal project, dedicated to the restoration of the Market, yet with the freedom of movement of a private body in obtaining mortgage backing.

Manring and Miller undertook the task of convincing city and federal officials that the proposed body would meet all legal requirements. Yale Lewis lobbied Olympia for state enabling authority allowing the city to establish such a corporation. John Miller, who had been elected to the city council in 1971 on a pro-Market initiative platform, sponsored the ordinance creating the Pike Place Market Preservation and Development Authority (PDA). Mayor Uhlman signed it, and the Preservation and Development Authority was chartered in June 1973.

The PDA has a twelve-member board, four appointed by the mayor, four by the Market Historical Commission, and four elected by the "constituency." The constituency was proposed as a means of encouraging public participation. Any Washington State resident can become a member of the Pike Place constituency after reaching the age of sixteen and paying a dollar a year membership fee. The Authority's mission is to purchase, rehabilitate, own, and manage property in the Pike Place Public Market.

The Historical Commission and the urban renewal staff sought answers: What is the Market we are trying to save? How do we go about it, technically and legally? Disagreement was inevitable, especially between Steinbrueck and the urban renewal people. Urban renewal had come to be equated with demolition. Steinbrueck wanted specifics. Wary of the free-swinging wrecking ball, he fought for a plan that would spell out, beyond the possibility of demolition-through-reinterpretation, the fate of each specific site in the historic district.

TOP: *Everybody wondered what was going on behind the plywood walls that went up during the rehabilitation work. Some signs proclaimed the new day acoming. (Photo by Nick Jahn)*

ABOVE: *Others pleaded that what was restored would be recognizable. (Pike Place Market News)*

FACING PAGE: *The Friends of the Market, though not in full accord among themselves, fought for their interpretation of the Initiative 1 victory. (Courtesy of Victor Steinbrueck)*

A proposed compromise was put together at a series of evening workshops at the Seattle Center, where the governing philosophy for the whole twenty-two acre renewal area was stated: "It is generally better to preserve than to repair, better to repair than to restore, better to restore than to reconstruct." As applied within the historic district, the plan called for the rehabilitation of twenty-four structures, the rehabilitation or replacement of seventeen others. The planners' map was a bureaucrat's dream world of arcane alphabetic symbols. Buildings and sites were identified as MCHRR (Mixed Commercial Historical District Rehabilitation/Replacement, which Steinbrueck translated as "It can be torn down"), R (Residential Area), MC (Mixed Commercial Area), MCHR (Mixed Commercial Historical District Rehabilitation Area, or "It cannot be torn down"), and P (Parking).

This was not specific enough for Steinbrueck. He opposed the compromise and the Friends of the Market backed him. The former members of the Alliance for a Living Market supported the plan. So, over Steinbrueck's dissent, did the Historical Commission. The city council went along with the majority point of view and approved the plan, adopting the Pike Place Project ordinance.

With the project plan at last in place, federal money could flow. Senator Warren G. Magnuson turned the spigot and the flow became a flood. During the initiative campaign, Maggie—as nearly everybody in Seattle called the Senator—had assured the Friends of the Market he would work to see that, if the measure passed, the $28,000,000 in urban renewal funds set aside for the Pike Place project would not be lost. When the initiative won, Maggie promised, "The people voted it. I will deliver it." Few doubted his ability to deliver. After all, Maggie's legislative legerdemain had financed the Seattle World Fair in 1962.

As chairman of the Senate Commerce Committee and second ranking member of the Appropriations Committee on which he chaired the Health Education Welfare and Labor Subcommittee, he had a major voice in just about every area of domestic policy if he chose to raise it. When Maggie talked, bureaucrats, including cabinet secretaries, listened. Now he raised his voice for the Market.

He let the Department of Housing and Urban Development know that the $28,000,000 earlier promised Seattle was to be delivered. Hesitation vanished,

the money moved west. It proved insufficient, so Maggie attached a rider to an appropriations bill setting up an "Urgent Needs" fund for cities suffering from the federal decision to change categorical grant programs into block grants. The rider provided the Pike Place Project with an additional $10,600,000. Another wave of Maggie's cigar and $2,000,000 materialized in low-interest rehabilitation loan funds. Then a $2,500,000 allocation of public works and street repair monies made possible the reconstruction of the Hillclimb Corridor between the Market and the waterfront. Finally, a Housing and Urban Development block grant appropriation was tapped for another

Implicit in the mandate for preservation of the Market and the change in concept of the urban renewal project was the idea that reconstruction would not be carried out by a single large developer, but by many developers and architects. It was also agreed that it was important to retain continuity. Contractors would find it more convenient to shut the Market down during rebuilding, but this would ruin small businesses without reserves. The Market would be remade piecemeal with different architects working on different projects.

George Bartholick, whose designs for Fairhaven College at Bellingham and the Woodland Park Zoo were much admired, drew a key assignment—the restoration of the L-shaped complex originally designed by Frank Goodwin in sketches on envelopes. Goodwin had not left many drawings of the original sixteen buildings in the Main Market, so Bartholick hired people like Billy King, a resident artist, to climb and crawl through recesses of the labyrinth and make sketches. From this work he completed a picture of the original, which became the basis for restoration. He resisted the temptation to modernize, choosing instead to follow Goodwin's utilitarian concepts. When, after thirty months' work and $14,000,000, the restoration was complete, Bartholick was delighted at occasional complaints by casual visitors that the Market didn't seem much changed. It wasn't—on the surface—but it met the codes and was restructured to last.

$6,000,000, leading Senator Proxmire to remark to Maggie, "That's some little market you've got out there, Senator."

The Market was remembered, too, in other appropriations reaching Seattle for citywide projects. Federal expenditures on the Pike Place Project came to between fifty and sixty million dollars, depending on who was counting and for what purpose. (Private investment in the project—tenant improvements and building capital—was estimated at seventy-five million.)

Rehabilitation of the Corner Market was assigned to Karlis Rekevics, a staff member of the city's urban renewal

ABOVE: *When the barriers came down, old-timers waited apprehensively to see what the restorers had done to the furniture of their lives. (Photo by Nick Jahn)*

FACING PAGE: *The skyline to the north was changing—the Silver Oakum had become the Triangle Building and had blossomed out with a Bolivian café, but grandmother had not been replaced by a chorus girl. (Photo by John Jeffcott)*

office. Fred Bassetti, one of the original Friends of the Market and a member of the University of Washington architecture faculty, transformed the old Triangle Building into seven one-bedroom apartments with Swedish balconies above commercial space fronting Pike Place. Arne Bystrom drew plans for the Seattle Garden Center, painted it apricot and trimmed it with "Bystrom green." Ibsen Nelson restored the Stewart House Apartments. Vic Steinbrueck, along with Richard Haag, landscaped the Market Park, renamed Steinbrueck Park, at the viewpoint where Western Avenue meets Virginia Street.

Some buildings were removed. First to go was Nellie Curtis's initial establishment in the Market area, the wood-frame Camp Hotel, officially known as the Salvation Army Building, after its final

occupant. Ninety-six housing units for low-income tenants occupy the site of the Camp and the adjoining Livingston Hotel. Nellie's other place, the LaSalle, has become a forty-unit low-income apartment house.

A city ordinance, championed by Victor Steinbrueck among others, allowed the conversion of the Stewart House, once destined for the wrecker's ball, into housing offering single rooms and a shared bathroom down the hall. Officially called "single room housing," it is unofficially known as "standing room only."

The Pike Place Market and Preservation Development Authority continued to acquire deeds to property within the historic district. It bought the Corner Market in 1975, the Soames/Dunn buildings and the Triangle Building in 1976, the Main Market and

the Economy Market in 1977, the Cliff House Hotel in 1979, and the Sanitary Market in 1980.

Twenty percent of the property in the historic district remained privately owned and was restored through private financing. The Fairmount Hotel was transformed into twenty-four apartments; the Butterworth and Alaska Trade buildings leased office space; the building housing the Seattle Garden Center and Sur La Table was improved by the owners; the new Olson-Walker Building at the corner of Pike Place and Virginia, became a condominium above a storefront delicatessen.

With a 1981 operating budget of $2,000,000, the Preservation and Development Authority combined landlord functions (once exercised by the Desimone family and other private owners) and the leasing of farmers' tables (formerly performed by the Market Master) with the operation of three parking lots on the water side of Western Avenue, control of the private security force, and development responsibility for the full twenty-two acre renewal project area.

ABOVE: *Even by Pike Place standards, the old St. Vincent de Paul was not an emporium noted for the excellence of its offerings. Still, there were bargains to be found. (University of Washington Libraries, Special Collections, Mary Randlett Collection)*

FACING PAGE, TOP: *The space occupied by a gas station and parking lot at the foot of Virginia Street has been transformed into Steinbrueck Park. Shoppers can picnic on the grass, check ferry schedules, and engage in the Olympic sport of mountain watching. (University of Washington Libraries, Special Collections, Mary Randlett Collection)*

FACING PAGE, BOTTOM: *Reincarnated as Sur La Table, the building is still packed with merchandise, higher priced, but appropriate to the Market setting. (Photo by Nick Jahn)*

Chapter 11 | THE MARKET IS SAVED~AGAIN

By winter of 1980, federal funds had dried up. Seattle's winter rains descended upon the Market. Even after $40 million in renovation, roofs leaked onto the tables of the daystall merchants, wastewater backed up in small floods, and the floor buckled in the Main Market Arcade. The Pike Place Market Preservation and Development Authority was barely breaking even. It was so short of cash that in January 1980 window washing was suspended for a year. Ronald Reagan won a landslide victory for President. In the 1980 nationwide Republican sweep, the Market's federal benefactor, Senator Warren G. Magnuson, was defeated and the flow of money from "the other Washington" evaporated.

By the time Magnuson left the Senate, the PDA had a portfolio of historic buildings purchased with his federal largesse: the Corner Market, Soames/Dunn, Cliff House, Sanitary Market, Economy Market, Main Market, and the Triangle buildings. Because the rents secured from merchants were inadequate to cover any major renovation costs, the PDA Council started looking for other funding sources.

Necessity became the mother of what seemed to be an invention. The PDA staff learned that nonprofit organizations with historic buildings around the country were raising money by "selling" tax depreciation rights to investors who were looking for depreciation write-offs permissible under the Internal Revenue Code. Safe harbor leases allowed purchasers to depreciate buildings over fifteen years and take those losses against their other income. Fearing it was too good to be true, the PDA Council sought and gained

reassurances from their legal counsel that the deal would not put the Market at risk.

On February 26, 1980, the PDA Council, after consulting with legal counsel, authorized its Executive Director John Clise to sell the depreciation rights to the Cliff House and Sanitary Market buildings on wrap-around real estate contracts. The PDA would lease the ground to the syndicators and continue to manage the property. The buildings went on the national tax-syndication market.

FACING PAGE: *Historic building depreciation rights to the Corner Market Building were sold by the PDA to Corner Market Limited Partnership. (University of Washington Libraries, Special Collections, photo by Mary Randlett, April 1985, Mary Randlett Collection)*

BELOW: *Even the Doric columns and building of the North Arcade, designed by Frank Goodwin, were "sold" by the PDA to the Urban Group in the tax-syndication transactions. (University of Washington Libraries, Special Collections, photo by Mary Randlett, April 1985, Mary Randlett Collection)*

One group of prospective investors looked particularly promising, even though they were quintessential outsiders. Or, perhaps they seemed so ideal *because* they so well personified Seattle's image of a New York investor, unable to distinguish a geoduck from a garage, but able to write very large checks. The two New York City lawyers, Arthur Malman and Martin Major, eventually became known to Market advocates as "Arty and Marty." They were trained in tax and real estate law. They organized investors, friends, and family members to form limited partnerships to purchase the Cliff House and Sanitary Market, with each serving as executive vice president.

It was not Arty and Marty's first phantom purchase. They had already closed a deal for Tacoma's historic Pantages Theater. Normally reluctant to follow the lead of their neighbor to the South, Seattle's leaders treated Arty and Marty's lengthy presentation on "equity syndication" as a siren song.

On April 22, 1980, the PDA Council authorized John Clise to enter into "tax sale" contracts with the New York syndicators on the Cliff House and Sanitary Market. The first infusion of badly needed funds was only $700,000. It was far short of providing what was necessary for Pike Market building renovation, but enticed the PDA into more negotiations with Arty and Marty and their associates.

In 1981, the PDA sold historic building depreciation rights to the Stewart House to Stewart House Associates; in 1983, the PDA entered into a similar deal involving the remaining eight buildings in the Pike Place Market historical district: the Fairley, Corner, and Economy Markets; the North Arcade; the LaSalle Hotel; the Leland-Bakery building, the Soames/Dunn buildings; and the Triangle building. The entities making

ABOVE: *This elderly man buying sweet carrots for "three bunches for a buck" was unaware the Sanitary Market Building around him had been sold by the PDA in "tax sale" contracts to New York syndicators, the Urban Group. (The Market Foundation; photo by Victor Gardaya)*

FACING PAGE: *New Yorkers, Arthur Malman and Martin Major, principals in the Urban Group, making an appearance at the Market. It wasn't long before Market devotees and most of Seattle referred to them as "Arty and Marty," and to their investor group as THUG, as Malman and Major attempted what was viewed by most observers as a takeover of the Market. (Seattle Weekly, December 13, 1989)*

By Eric Scigliano

WHILE NEW YORKERS FRET OVER THE sale of Rockefeller Center to Japanese investors, Seattle is shaking its head over the apparent sale of an even more cherished institution to *New York* investors. No satirist could conceive so bizarre and piquant a milestone in Seattle's ascension to the status of happiest hunting ground for real estate speculators. For nine years, no one bothered to notice that the city had signed over to a savvy investment group, for a measly $3 million, Seattle's dearest repository of history, heirlooms, and humanity.

Martin Major, executive vice president of the Urban Group, made the rounds again last week reassuring all who would listen that the Market will never be lost to Seattle—even though the partnerships that he represents are suddenly asserting stringent authority over what they call "our property" and everyone in Seattle always called simply "our Market." One reassurance is certain: the Market's buildings, which barely manage to stand up where they are and are protected by a historical-district overlay, can never be hauled off, like a London Bridge, to Arizona.

Beyond that lie painful questions: just what *did* the Urban Group buy in 1980 and 1983, while everyone was looking and no one was watching? What changes will they try to enforce, in their newly revealed quest for short- and long-term profits, on a complex economic and social organism that has been dedicated to every purpose *except* profits?

Urban's Malman and Major in the Market: suddenly it's 'our property.'

the deals varied. There was the Corner Market Limited Partnership, the Pike Market Limited Partnership, the Pike Management Corporation, the Urban Investors Corporation, and the Livingston Baker Limited Partnership. Each time, the suitor had a different name, but all of the syndication schemes were limited partnerships assembled by Arty and Marty.

By January 1984, the deals collectively did not seem at all phantom-like. Malman and Major, with each of the limited partnerships under an umbrella corporation, the Urban Group, had gained title to eleven buildings in the Pike Place Market historical district, conveyed through a thousand pages of legal documents including ground leases, improvement leases, deeds of trust, sales agreements, and management contracts.

The Urban Group had gained a controlling interest in 90 percent of the Pike Place Market—420,000 of the 470,000 square feet managed by the Pike Place Market Preservation and Development Authority. There was no sign that any PDA Council or staff member, Market merchant, or citizen had any concern over what had transpired. If anything, the

glee over the Market's good fortune had grown over the years since Arty and Marty had come onto the scene.

The total purchase price of the three buildings and the leases on the other eight buildings was just over $21 million. The PDA, once desperately short of cash, received $2.93 million as a down payment in the deal and the Urban Group got its tax benefits. For several years, this marriage of convenience worked fine. The PDA charged merchants to cover operating costs and paid the Urban Group the token sum of $3,000 a year in annual rent. The PDA always assumed that when the time came in 1999 for the Urban Group to make balloon payments totaling $17 million, they would simply walk away from the deal, having been enriched by the tax benefits. This default on the balloon payment would terminate the lease options and restore ownership and control of the eleven buildings to the Pike Place Market Preservation and Development Authority.

But, once again events in Washington, D.C., changed the outlook for the Pike Place Market. The Tax Reform Act of 1986 was a sweeping modification to the Internal Revenue Code. Tax rates for the wealthiest of individuals were cut significantly. To help cover the federal government's revenue losses, numerous tax shelters were limited or closed, among them tax depreciation write-offs that the Urban Group and Pike Place Market had come to know and love.

By 1988, the changes in the Urban Group's behavior began to worry Pike Place Market PDA Executive Director Michael Carroll. In June 1988, Major sent a letter to the PDA stating that the Urban Group partners intended to refinance their mortgage on the Pike Place Market (five limited partnerships in eleven buildings) and demanding year-end financial information. He outlined the possibilities for a "favorable refinancing" due to low interest rates. The news shocked Carroll. As he understood it, the syndication deal meant the Urban Group had no interest in really "buying" the Pike Market and would default in a few years. Carroll wrote to Major, "it was our opinion that refinancing ran counter to the intent of the original framers of the syndication agreement, with the obvious exception of yourself."

The Urban Group was not dissuaded. In July 1989, it brought in the Arthur Anderson Company to audit the PDA's revenues and expenses related to the Cliff House, Sanitary Market, Stewart House, and Corner Market. As the auditors descended on the PDA offices tucked into Post Alley, Carroll, by now physically ill, suffering ulcers and loss of sleep, sent his first distress signal. He called a local architect into his office.

Luckily for Carroll and for the City of Seattle, it wasn't just any architect. It was Peter Steinbrueck, Victor's son. Peter was the Seattleite most likely to take the Urban Group's efforts seriously, and the most likely to take the efforts personally. Carroll was blunt. "These guys want to take over the Market," he told Steinbrueck. He carefully outlined for Steinbrueck the refinancing plans, the audit, and the letters describing the Urban Group's interpretation of the syndication as an actual purchase and sale.

Peter was every bit as tenacious as his father and he would prove to share Victor's scrappiness as well. He could not have been more earnest, a trait well received by the older Market vendors. At thirty-one he had already led the successful 1989 Citizens Alternative Plan (CAP) initiative campaign limiting building heights in downtown Seattle. Activists knew to call him and they had not been disappointed.

Peter was Victor and Elaine Steinbrueck's youngest child. He spent much of his childhood with his father at the Pike Place Market, eating big breakfasts at the Athenian, followed by sketching excursions, and talks with merchants and farmers. Peter spent one summer in 1970 at a daystall selling Friends of the Market buttons, posters, postcards, and books. Like the best farmer making an artful display of vegetables, he rearranged the buttons and Pike Market memorabilia several times a day. "I tried my best to sell as many buttons and postcards as I could, and blend in with the farmers and other daystallers." An eighth grade paper Peter wrote for an English class at Lakeside School told of the vendors who gave the Market its life: a sixty-five year old widow selling leather wallets, a partly crippled grandmother with her resplendent flowers, a woman rancher marketing eggs and rabbits on Saturday only, and a Yugoslav immigrant named Victor who regaled visitors with stories of the young Cassius Clay before he became boxing legend Mohammed Ali.

Peter learned at his father's side as he drew sketches with his fat Mont Blanc pen for *Market Sketchbook* and organized and designed the initial strategy to preserve the historic buildings and atmosphere of the Pike Place Market.

At the age of thirteen, Peter gathered signatures for the Friends of the Market initiative campaign. By 1983, he was ready for a more formal role as a Market guardian. Two years before Victor's death, Peter, nominated by his father, accepted a mayoral appointment to the Market Historical Commission. It was just as the Pike Place Market Preservation and Development Authority was signing papers to "sell" the Market buildings to the Urban Group.

Months after Michael Carroll's meeting with Peter Steinbrueck came the first public warning shot that signaled the conflict to come. Arthur Malman, speaking for the Urban Group, announced that it wanted to refinance its $20 million plus debt to "take advantage of reasonable interest rates." Malman acknowledged that the 1986 changes in tax law had soured their investment in the Pike Place Market.

Critics of the Urban Group treated Malman's proclamation as the most

unpleasant of surprises, saying it was the first time Arty and Marty had revealed that their investment wasn't solely related to tax shelters. The critics encapsulated their dissatisfaction by renaming the Urban Group "THUG," an acrimonious acronym that would stick with the Seattle media and Market advocates for years to come. There was no sign that Malman was amused. He presented the cold figures. The Urban Group had put $3 million into the Market and was carrying a $20 million debt. To date it had received a single $5,000 check and that was five years past. He also unpleasantly revealed that the Urban Group had hired the Arthur Anderson Company to probe the PDA management, or mismanagement, of the Pike Place Market.

Seattle newspapers finally woke up to the real estate transactions and the threat to public ownership of the Pike Place

BELOW: *It was sometimes possible for Peter Steinbrueck to muster a smile during the early days of the fight with the Urban Group over ownership of the Market. As the fight dragged on, Steinbrueck found little to smile about and not much time for levity. (Courtesy of Peter Steinbrueck)*

Market. The *Seattle Weekly* warned that the control of the Market was the issue and that the seriousness of the Urban Group's intentions was underscored by them retaining Gogerty and Stark, a political consulting firm. One of the prominent principals of the firm was former Seattle deputy mayor Bob Gogerty, thought prior to that point to be an ally of the Market preservationists. Further media eyebrows were raised as the Urban Group moved to retain Bogle & Gates, Seattle's closest approximation to a silk stocking law firm.

Members of the Friends of the Market network had plenty to worry about, and worry they did. They called upon Victor Steinbrueck's son, to see what Peter could do. Steinbrueck and his friend, Peter Eglick, a Seattle land-use attorney, prepared for action by poring over all one thousand pages of documents describing the transactions between the PDA and the Urban Group.

Soon afterward, when Peter went to the Pike Place Market to attend an Historical Commission meeting, he met an old woman who lived in a low-income housing unit. The woman said to him, "They've sold the Market." The more time Steinbrueck spent with the real estate document, the more he began to think that she was absolutely right. Peter allowed himself to think that there were safeguards that would temper what seemed to be the documents' clear meaning.

The safeguards were not to be found. On November 23, an agitated Steinbrueck went public with a letter to the *Seattle Post-Intelligencer*, under the headline, "Pike Place Market Sold to New York Syndicate." Steinbrueck, seen as the

ABOVE: *Confusion and contradictory information ruled the day as the battle between the Urban Group and the City of Seattle grew. "There's an awful lot of talk but no one seems to know the facts," said Trudy Barkley, a Market merchant. (Seattle Times file, 1989)*

FACING PAGE: *The Citizens Alliance had a hand-drawn button, reminiscent of the Friends of the Market buttons. To keep it simple, there was only one button in this campaign. (Courtesy of Peter Steinbrueck)*

City's Market watchdog, was unequivocal in his rendering of the bad news:

> Yes, it really is true. All the buildings in the Market once held in the public trust by the Pike Place Market Preservation and Development Authority were sold by the PDA to a New York-based private investment syndicate. It is not known at this time what the outcome of the financial audit will be, but one thing is certain: these complicated legal agreements raise very serious questions about how these decisions were made, and what unseen hands may be affecting the management and character of the Market.

The claims and counterclaims intensified. The *Seattle Times* headlined, "Will New York Investors Take Over Pike Market?" Ominously, *Times* reporter Robert T. Nelson quoted Arty and Marty as saying "an audit of the Market's PDA . . . may conclude that investors are owed $6 million to $8 million in back earnings from their purchase of 11 buildings in the district." The *Times* added it was the changes in the Tax Reform Act of 1986 that were motivating the Urban Group to seek to become "permanent fixtures." On the defensive, PDA officials reacted by saying this was strictly a tax benefit transaction, that the Urban Group had never "owned" the market nor cared about expenses and revenues.

In the heart of the market, at the daystalls, the merchants' rumor mill grew. Never fond of the PDA, merchants feared the worst. The talk at the daystalls and the shops was that the PDA had sold the Market out from under the public, rents would be going up, and that the Market's world was coming to an end.

Some civic leaders counseled calm. The *Times* editorialized: "Investors, PDA Can Work Out Differences." The *Times*

editors said that there was plenty of common ground, the opportunity for compromise was encouraging and there was "too much at stake to allow the agreements to unravel or, worse, to wind up in court."

Down the hall at the same newspaper, colorful *Times* columnist Rick Anderson didn't feel that way. Two days later his column bitterly criticized the Urban Group under the headline: "Goodbye Pike Place Market; Hello N.Y. Theme Park." Anderson predicted "Harry's All-Night Deli and New York Theme Park." Referring to "capitalist running dogs," Anderson predicted a "New York–style welcoming sign, 'eat or I'll kill you' and food concessions—New York pizza, New York bagels and New York seltzer." Other elements were "thrill rides," "loud mouth land," "animal park," "mugville," and a host of other New York horrors.

Even though the primary heat was on the Urban Group, there was plenty left over for what some saw as the PDA's considerable failings. At a packed meeting between Arthur Malman, the PDA officials, and the public on December 12, Peter Steinbrueck was pointed: "The PDA was a trustee of the City of Seattle . . . they had no right to sell it." The crowd's central question was "Who sold the Pike Place Market?" Their consternation shifted the focus momentarily from the Urban Group to John Clise and Harris Hoffman

---

ABOVE: *Cartoons featuring the Urban Group at the Pike Place Market illustrated editorial pages of Seattle's daily newspapers during this era. This cartoon created by Steve Greenberg appeared in the* Seattle Post-Intelligencer, *January 22, 1990. (Copyright Steve Greenberg)*

FACING PAGE: *Peter Steinbrueck found himself in the company of a multitude of lawyers, as many of Seattle's finest attorneys stepped forward to volunteer their services in defense of public ownership of the Market. Here, second on Steinbrueck's left is attorney Jackson Schmidt, who argued the theory of "ultra vires" prevented the sale of the Market to a private entity such as the Urban Group. (The Market Foundation)*

who signed the agreements as the PDA Executive Directors.

After the meeting, *Post-Intelligencer* editorialists joined their daily newspaper competitor in arguing that the dispute should be resolved through negotiation, not by lawsuit. Steinbrueck doubted that approach would be successful, feeling that the negotiation position of Seattle and the PDA would be weakened by their involvement with Arty, Marty, and the Urban Group from the beginning.

Columnist Rick Anderson believed that attention to the PDA's past or present shortcomings would doom the Market. "Don't let them divide and conquer," he insisted, and then, more graphically, "We can kick the PDA's butt later . . . " He accused the Urban Group of both guaranteeing that they weren't going to raise rents and then announcing that was exactly what they were going to do. Anderson focused on the question most on the minds of Market followers. "What do the New York owners of the Market want?"

Thus the battle shifted from who sold the Market and why to what it would take to make the Urban Group go away. Pike Market officials had concluded that the Urban Group's paramount goal was "greenmail," a deliberate effort to stir up enough public anxiety so that they would be bought out. If anxiety was the short-term goal, the Urban Group was experiencing nothing but success.

Steinbrueck knew that a new strategy was required and he was not keen on the Pike Place Market Preservation and Development Authority being at the center of its development. Instead, Market advocates would come to benefit from a group of talented Seattle lawyers stepping forward. The legal team that Steinbrueck and others sought emerged from the best law firms in Seattle and they donated

hundreds of thousands of dollars worth of time. They began attending meetings on strategy, led initially by Peter Eglick and Samuel Jacobs, the lawyer who worked with Steinbrueck on the CAP initiative. Dan Pepple, a contracts and transactions attorney and partner in Gordon, Thomas, Honeywell, Malanca, Peterson & Daheim, was a veteran of the same sort of tax-syndication deals and thus was mortally certain that they were never intended to permanently transfer property ownership.

The lawyers tested theories on each other. Eglick suggested "ultra vires," a contracts theory disparaged as outdated and arcane in law school, but awfully enticing to the group of beleaguered lawyers looking to save the Market. Gordon Thomas associate Jackson Schmidt was released from other cases and was deployed to the King County Courthouse library. In one week's time, he prepared a memo and returned to the legal team. To his surprise, Schmidt was able to say clearly and firmly, "We have a viable legal theory." Schmidt said that an ultra vires contract is one that "is outside the authority of a municipal corporation to enter."

Ultra vires was designed to protect citizens and taxpayers from unjust, ill-considered, or extortionate contracts. The young lawyer believed that the PDA did not have the authority in its charter to

give away its power to manage the Market buildings according to the purposes voted on by the Seattle citizens setting up the Pike Place Market Historical District Ordinance. If he and the legal team were right, the contract would be unenforceable and the Urban Group would be stymied.

Steinbrueck set up a nonprofit organization to lead the legal fight. Copying the successful Friends of the Market model, he established the Citizens Alliance to Keep the Pike Place Market Public. Appropriately, the Citizens Alliance set up shop in donated space in the heart of the Market, upstairs in the Champion Building at 1928 Pike Place. Member organizations included Allied Arts, Friends of the Market, Market Constituency, Market Merchants Association, Market Foundation, Meat Cutters Local #81, Washington Trust for Historic Preservation, and the Metropolitan Democratic Club. As the legal team prepared an outline for the assault in court, two law firms offered the

Citizens Alliance pro bono support for the case: Gordon, Thomas, Honeywell, Malanca, Peterson & Daheim (Daniel P. Pepple and Jackson Schmidt) and Keller Rohrback (Len Barson).

The efforts of the legal team were not devoted solely to the preparation of briefs. Volunteer attorney William Knowles' research was put to music, performed by Broken Statue and set to the tune of the Kingston Trio's "M. T. A.," as "The Pike Place Market Rag" with lyrics beginning:

> Let me tell you a story 'bout the Pike Place Market / and its sad condition today.
> In 1970 it was bought by the people/and entrusted to the PDA.

ABOVE: *Protestors took to the street, marching down Pike Place carrying signs, "Keep the Public Market Public" and "Say No to NY," to keep the Market in public hands and out of the control of the Urban Group. (Seattle Times* file, 1990, *photo by Barry Wong)*

Well now, people of Seattle/
don't you think it's a scandal
    that they gave our Market away?/
Stop the rent increases.
    Oust the Urban Group/and let
the public run the PDA.

Lifted by the lawyers, Steinbrueck decided he wanted a show of force to let the New Yorkers see they were up against a formidable opponent. On March 7, 1990, the Citizens Alliance took their boldest position. Flanked by a ten-person legal team at the Pike Place Market Senior Center, Steinbrueck announced at a press conference that the Citizens Alliance would file suit unless the PDA and the Urban Group investors terminated the relationship and all transactions. One hundred people marched down Pike Place waving banners "Keep the Pike Public Market Public." A black plastic shroud was draped over the word "public" on the Public Market Center sign.

Steinbrueck did not want the Citizens Alliance to take on the Urban Group and the Pike Place Market Preservation and Development Authority alone. Even with the large legal team, expenses could be prohibitive, so he sought access to the City of Seattle's deeper pockets. Over salad in a Smith Tower restaurant, Steinbrueck and Peter Eglick laid out their planned ultra vires contract-voiding offensive to Seattle City Attorney Mark Sidran. Perhaps in part because of the City's own potential exposure to claims that the transactions were illegal, Sidran agreed to expand the home team. He brought the City's considerable legal resources into an informal partnership with the Alliance and the PDA.

The Preservation and Development Authority joined the Citizens Alliance in seeking big league help in its own fight with the Urban Group. As its legal

counsel, the PDA retained Preston Gates & Ellis, a Seattle law firm founded in 1883, fourteen years before the Pike Place Market opened. Preston Gates' lead lawyer for the PDA was B. Gerald "Gerry" Johnson. Johnson was a Seattle native and former chief of staff to Senator Warren G. Magnuson. A graduate of Roosevelt High School, Dartmouth College, and Georgetown Law School, Johnson gathered signatures for the Friends of the Market initiative campaign while home from college, accompanied Senator Magnuson as he walked through the Market on congressional breaks, and was Magnuson's staff member responsible for obtaining funding for the Pike Place Market in the Senate Appropriations Subcommittee on HUD. and Independent agencies.

Johnson knew power and power politics. He saw the Urban Group's actions and requested that the PDA bring in a tough negotiator to lead discussions with the Urban Group. In January 1990, on Johnson's advice, the PDA turned to former Seattle deputy mayor Shelly Yapp to manage its negotiations with the New Yorkers. It would be a great understatement to say that Shelly Yapp's reputation preceded her. No one in Seattle displayed more backbone. She was smart, strong-willed, quick-witted, and, if necessary, her bemused smile could vanish in an instant. This was a force with which one would not choose to trifle.

Yapp had been deputy mayor to Mayor Charles Royer and budget director to King County Executive Randy Revelle (Tom Revelle's great grandson). Anne Fennessey, Royer's communications director said of Yapp, "She doesn't destroy things, but she doesn't let anything get in her way." Merchants who dealt with Yapp in her later years as PDA director considered her almost impossibly difficult

to deal with at times. As Yapp said when the battles with the Urban Group were concluded, "Now we can go back to fighting with each other."

Soon after taking on the lead negotiator job, Yapp called Steinbrueck and the two met for coffee at the Market. Steinbrueck was encouraged. He found an ally with fighting spirit. He said, "She came in bat swinging, ready to take on the Urban Group. She was talking tough, not ready to compromise."

The Preston Gates legal team for the PDA reorganized into litigation mode. Gerry Johnson remained lead strategist and general counsel to the PDA. Johnson

turned to Fred Tausend, a native of New York City who had joined Preston Gates in January 1990, just months earlier. Tausend was former dean of the Seattle University law school, a civil liberties activist, and a superb trial attorney. Tausend would argue the Market's case in the courtroom.

While Yapp began talks with the Urban Group, the city and the PDA filed separate lawsuits against the Urban Group in King County Superior Court. In April 1990, the Citizens Alliance filed its lawsuit against the PDA and the Urban Group in King County Superior Court. The claim of all three lawsuits was the same; the statutes and regulations which created the PDA gave it the power and the duty to preserve and manage the Market in the interests of the people of Seattle, a responsibility that could not be given away. The Citizens' lawsuit asserted three claims: (1) the "ultra vires" theory, that the PDA exceeded its authority by entering into agreements that would divest the PDA of management of the Market; (2) the transactions between the PDA and the Urban Group were really a sham entered into for tax benefits only and were never intended to be an actual sale; and (3) the deals were a "lending of municipal credit" prohibited under the constitution of the state of Washington. The case was assigned to Judge Frank Sullivan, a long-time Seattle public servant.

On May 30, 1990, the Urban Group responded to the City, PDA, and Citizens Alliance suits, asking Judge Sullivan to appoint a receiver to act in the place of the PDA alleging that its mismanagement had damaged the Market and the Urban Group. Arty, Marty, and their colleagues wanted $5 million for losses they claimed had been caused by PDA mismanagement, damages for slander and defamation, and court orders requiring the Urban Group approval for any significant PDA actions regarding Market leases and physical changes. Shelly Yapp said to Tausend, "We have to have a victory." Tausend and the Preston Gates team worked over the Fourth of July holiday preparing briefs for the PDA. Tausend, and his partner Paul Lawrence, appeared before Judge Sullivan in King County Superior Court arguing that the Pike

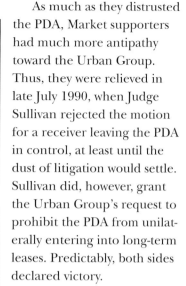

Place Market should not be placed in the hands of a receiver.

As much as they distrusted the PDA, Market supporters had much more antipathy toward the Urban Group. Thus, they were relieved in late July 1990, when Judge Sullivan rejected the motion for a receiver leaving the PDA in control, at least until the dust of litigation would settle. Sullivan did, however, grant the Urban Group's request to prohibit the PDA from unilaterally entering into long-term leases. Predictably, both sides declared victory.

On October 31, 1990, Judge Sullivan greeted all the lawyers with "a happy Halloween to all of you." But, the Urban Group would be getting a trick rather than a treat. In his oral ruling, Judge Sullivan rejected most of the Urban Group's legal

---

FACING PAGE: *Creative protest against the New Yorkers and the Urban Group resulted in the shrouding of the "Public" portion of the Market's famous neon sign, Public Market Center. "Market Center," said one observer, "sounds like a grocery store." (Seattle Times file, 1990, photo by Angela Gottshalk)*

ABOVE, TOP: *Gerry Johnson worked with Senator Warren G. Magnuson as he obtained federal funds for the Market; toured the Market with the Senator on breaks; and returned to Seattle to lead the legal battle, heading up the Preston Gates & Ellis defense of the PDA in its fight with the Urban Group. (Courtesy of Preston Gates & Ellis)*

ABOVE: *Fred Tausend, a native New Yorker, led the Preston Gates & Ellis courtroom team to argue the case for the Market. "This was the most important case of my lifetime," said Tausend. (Courtesy of Preston Gates & Ellis)*

claims. Most importantly, he agreed with the Citizens' "ultra vires" argument that the PDA did not have the authority to delegate its functions. Only the City had the power to remove the PDA as market manager, not the Urban Group.

That was just the beginning. Sullivan also held: the PDA could determine how much of the maintenance and operation costs of running the Market could be passed on to the Urban Group, the Market was not required to charge market rates for space it rented, and the city would not have to pay any damages the Urban Group might assert against the PDA. The latter ruling signaled the New Yorkers that they would have difficulty finding someone

ABOVE: *Shelly Yapp tours the Market after the Christmas holiday in 1989. Yapp was hired by the PDA to negotiate with the Urban Group. Yapp, known to be very tough, was unrelenting in the clash with the principals of the Urban Group and their attorneys.* (Seattle Times *file, 1989, photo by Benjamin Benschneider)

to write the check even if their damage claims ultimately prevailed.

The oral ruling was so overwhelmingly in favor of the Citizens Alliance, the PDA, and the City of Seattle, that Peter Steinbrueck found himself, "nearly speechless." This condition did not last long, as he moved to extend the Urban Group's bad dreams from Judge Sullivan's Halloween nightmare. Steinbrueck and the Citizens Alliance were not the only source. The day after Halloween, the law firm of Bogle & Gates, owed hundreds of thousands of dollars by the Urban Group, notified Judge Sullivan of its intent to withdraw from the case as soon as another attorney could be found.

The Urban Group was becoming increasingly desperate. It filed a petition for Chapter 11 bankruptcy in the New York court in late November. This new action was intended in part to slow Judge Sullivan down now that he had made his intentions clear. The bankruptcy petition stayed Judge Sullivan's oral rulings and prevented the entry of a formal written order enforcing those rulings. Perhaps as important, the action also allowed the Urban Group to obtain a new attorney without paying Bogle & Gates and seek what could be a heretofore unavailable "home court advantage" in a New York courtroom.

The Southern District of New York Bankruptcy Court is an imposing structure. Located in the old Customs Building on the southern tip of Manhattan, it had been the entrance to the United States for Joe Desimone and other immigrants who moved west to Seattle and the Pike Market. Through the window behind Senior Judge Cornelius Blackshear, Seattle attorneys could see the Statue of Liberty.

Fred Tausend, attorney for the PDA and the Citizens Alliance, described the scene:

The day of the hearing was the day Pan American Airlines filed for bankruptcy. They held the planes in the air. Pan Am airplanes were circling overhead waiting for a decision when Judge Blackshear came out. We were the first on his docket, Pan Am was second. Judge Blackshear immediately saw what was coming after the Pike Place Market case. Hundreds of attorneys for the airline industry and creditors packed the courtroom.

Tausend and City Attorney Mark Sidran each gave an oral argument. Tausend spent his twenty minutes giving Judge Blackshear a quick history of public markets in Los Angeles and New York; how they disappeared; the 1970s' initiative campaign in Seattle, led by Victor Steinbrueck; the renovation of the Pike Market through the tax-credit deals with the Urban Group and the resultant litigation. Tausend described the litigation leading to bankruptcy court. He showed photographs from 1907 to the present day and he quoted farmers, street musicians, fishmongers, and elderly residents.

Tausend recalled, "I wanted Judge Blackshear to understand the asset he would be dealing with. This is not just any real estate. The Pike Place Public Market is the soul of Seattle."

The Seattle lawyers asked the judge to: (1) dismiss the bankruptcy case as a bad faith filing to avoid the litigation in progress, and (2) transfer the case to the federal bankruptcy court in Seattle. To the latter plea, the New York bankruptcy judge agreed, causing Mark Sidran to remark, "we feel at least like we took a bite out of the Big Apple." The case was transferred and assigned to Bankruptcy Court Judge Frank Howard in Seattle. Judge Howard had served with Judge Sullivan as a King County Superior Court Judge

and joined the Bankruptcy Court after his retirement.

The Urban Group's once bright prospects were dimming at every turn. They made an offer to the Citizens Alliance to "buy" a one-third interest in the Urban Group's Market holdings for $1.5 million, with no money down. The offer was quickly rejected. Steinbrueck and his colleagues reasoned, since the Urban Group didn't own anything, what was there to buy? Next, the Urban Group asked Judge Howard to appoint a private manager for the Market, the same tactic unsuccessfully employed with Judge Sullivan. They also revealed that title companies who had insured the PDA purchase and lease transactions had refused to pay the Bogle & Gates litigation costs, now totaling nearly a million dollars.

The Urban Group's bankruptcy claim was the New York investors' last hope. The Market lawyers continued to seek the dismissal of the bankruptcy proceeding as being in "bad faith." Now exhausted, both sides waited for Judge Howard's decision, the Market forces hoping for a knockout blow, coming in part from a mandated return to the friendly venue of Judge Sullivan's Superior Courtroom, previously the scene of Halloween greetings.

Judge Howard's May 16, 1991, ruling did not end the conflict, but it set it up for its final round. He lifted the stay on the proceedings before Judge Sullivan, a significant victory for Market forces because that meant all Sullivan's favorable oral rulings would be enforced very shortly. However, Howard declined to dismiss the bankruptcy case entirely, a move which the Urban Group's new attorney, William Weinstein, claimed as a victory. Significantly, Weinstein went public with his suggestion that the parties settle the case because "the PDA and the city are generating more in legal fees on a monthly basis than the amount of money it would take to settle this case."

The signal was not lost on Shelly Yapp, who renewed her efforts. Within a month, both the *Seattle Post-Intelligencer* and the *Times* reported that the parties were close to settling the lawsuit, ending all of the Urban Group's claims to the Market and guaranteeing it remain under public management. The settlement deal was first reported to involve payment of $2.5 million to the Urban Group to get them to go away. The main obstacle was said to be how the PDA was to come up with the cash, but the deal got a good deal stickier when the Market merchants learned it was in the works. As *Times* reporter Nelson put it, "it's hard to tell which the Pike Place tenants dislike the most—the PDA . . . or the settlement with the New York investors."

The old suspicions about the PDA selling the farmers, merchants, and crafts folks out, raising rents to pay the settlement amount, led to a last rebellion. "This is about what you'd expect from the scumbags who sold the Market to the Urban Group in the first place," said one merchant. "We want no deals with the Urban Group," insisted another. Added to the opponents of a settlement was the Urban Group creditor Bogle & Gates, which maintained it must be paid more than $600,000 before any settlement could be approved by the court. Gogerty & Stark, along with Arthur Anderson Inc., were also creditors who could demand payment as a condition to settlement. As combatants debated, costs continued to rise.

The sentiment for settlement continued to be mixed. The City Council chair Paul Kraabel said "it sounds like a potentially good thing." Local Democratic legislators entered the battle, suggesting that the state might help the PDA out by appropriating $2 million towards the set-

tlement, since the Market was of statewide significance. Some Republicans weighed in, calling it Seattle's "problem." Local ferment continued until Steinbrueck and the Citizens Alliance agreed to the settlement. There were two conditions: (1) the settlement agreement provides for reform of the market's governing procedures, and (2) the parties guarantee that money to pay off the Urban Group not come from the Market's merchants.

The month of June was spent in search of settlement money far removed from the merchant's pockets. The Market parties (by now, the Citizens Alliance, PDA, and the City of Seattle working in concert) joined in lobbying the Washington State Legislature for help. It was a difficult sell. Many Eastern Washington legislators were concerned that too much money was already going west of the Cascade Mountains. If Seattle's PDA made the mistake of getting into the syndication mess, why should the whole state of Washington bail the Market out?

Shelly Yapp and the ever-present lawyers met with Washington House Speaker Joe King and Appropriations Committee chair Helen Sommers. Sommers and King wrote a proposal for the House. Senator Ray Moore, a Pike Place Market advocate worked nights and weekends to forge a compromise. On June 29, 1991, during the final days of a special session, the House and Senate approved a state grant of $1.5 million for the Pike Place Market settlement, on the understandable condition that the PDA charter be changed to prohibit sales of interests in Market properties ever again.

At a public meeting on June 28, despite cries of "scam," the PDA council voted 8–4 to accept the settlement. On July 8, all parties declared peace. The settlement was deceptively simple. In essence, the Urban Group received $2.25

million in exchange for giving up all right, title, and interest to anything in the Pike Place Market. The Urban Group also settled with a group of title companies and received $750,000.

In the end, Seattle citizens kept their Market. Beyond the people, the battle benefited no one but the lawyers who were compensated. Too good to be true, turned out to be not so good at all. The PDA received its initial $3 million in 1981, badly needed money which was put to good use, but they lost a great deal of the public's confidence and paid a huge attorney bill. The Urban Group, which put up $3 million in 1981, received $2.25 million back from the PDA in the settlement, another $750,000 from title insurance companies, and got an estimated $7 million in tax benefits. But the Urban Group, like the PDA and the City, paid gross amounts in attorney fees and other expenses. And they were forced to walk away from the property they had coveted.

On October 11, 1991, nearly a year after the Halloween ruling by Judge Sullivan and over two years since Michael Carroll sounded the warning, Peter Steinbrueck received a fax. It was a memo from attorney Gerry Johnson titled "settlement." "Arthur and Marty signed this morning. The Market parties are signing this afternoon and Monday." Johnson asked Steinbrueck and twenty-five others from the Market legal team to join in an impromptu afternoon celebration. Now joining Victor Steinbrueck on the list of Market heroes—Shelly Yapp, Gerry Johnson, Fred Tausend, Paul Lawrence, Jackson Schmidt, Len Barson, Peter Steinbrueck, and the now customary room full of lawyers. At 3:30 P.M., on the seventy-fifth floor of the Columbia Tower, they raised their glasses, looked out toward Puget Sound and the Pike Place Public Market, and knew that the Market had been saved. Again.

ABOVE: *Shelly Yapp found herself not only in a difficult dialogue with the Urban Group and its representatives, but also spending a great deal of time dealing with disgruntled Market merchants, farmers, and other Market interests. Many of the public meetings were lengthy and heated. (Seattle Times file, 1990, photo by Craig Fujii)*

Chapter 12 | TENDING TO THE CITY'S SOUL

Two battles, only twenty years apart, saved the Pike Place Market and its buildings. Seattle had a downtown market and farmers and merchants were provided a place to sell their wares. But some said it was the soul of Seattle that had been saved.

After the passage of the 1971 initiative, those who loved the Market began to examine the needs of the downtown residents for whom the Market was virtually a home. The initiative required the Market to develop social and other services, but the capacity to do so was absent. As George Rolfe, Director of the PDA, recalled, "We didn't know what was meant by public services and didn't really know what people needed. We were looking for someone to work with the *farmers*. We had to be convinced to work with the *residents*." Yet again, the PDA found the right person at the right time. The "someone" who would develop the essential new programs turned out to be Aaron Zaretsky.

Zaretsky, who would become Executive Director of the Market Foundation in 1982, joined the PDA staff in 1977. His passion was to create a sense of community in the Market's residential neighborhood and thereby to ensure the Market's stability. "His efforts were to even the score between the people and the buildings," recalls Chris Hurley, who worked with Zaretsky and later became the first Director of the Pike Market Clinic. The task of focusing on the people—the neighborhood's many low-income residents—was all the more daunting because it faced strong opposition from key community figures who had been involved in the Market's renovation.

Zaretsky insisted the PDA could develop a new, more productive relationship with the neighborhood's residential population. His first task was to find out exactly who lived downtown. He found that more than half of the 20,000 downtown residents were elderly, poor, disabled, or alone, but *not* transients. Zaretsky discovered that nearly all downtown–social services were addressing the highly visible, and certainly needy, transient populations, but were not meeting the needs of downtown's senior citizens.

In the absence of a neighborhood association, Zaretsky and his colleagues created one. They invited people in the community to come together to discuss their needs. Much to their surprise, over fifty people came to the first meeting. To their even greater surprise most were residents, some were Market merchants, and

ABOVE: *Aaron Zaretsky and Chris Hurley, hired by the PDA to "even the score between the people of the Market and its buildings," conducted research, held meetings with residents, and developed services for downtown residents living near the Market. Zaretsky became the first executive director of the Market Foundation and Hurley, the first director of the Pike Market Clinic. (The Market Foundation)*

FACING PAGE: *Rachel's image surveys Puget Sound and the Public Market sign transformed for a Market Foundation campaign, "Care for the Market." (The Market Foundation)*

virtually all shared Zaretsky's belief that the Market had unmet obligations. A core group of about thirty met regularly, dreaming of new agencies to serve the community. They identified problems, generated ideas, and assessed demand for services.

They understood local health care needs and immediately started the planning for a community clinic. But they also learned about the value of a five-cent cup of coffee. Before renovation, the Market had always been a place where people, especially older people, could gather and linger much of the day over coffee. Whatever their past preference, area residents were united in one desire moving forward. 96 percent of the people responding to the planning committee's questionnaire wanted to see a community center established in the Market area to give them a new place to pass the time of day.

The sheer number of downtown residents struggling to make ends meet stimulated a plan for a food bank. The fourth need became obvious as Zaretsky wandered the Market. He explains, "Inexpensive day care was a real problem and it wasn't unusual to find kids bundled up at the day tables in winter while their parents were selling. Working people often faced the choice of quitting a job or taking the kids along." A child care center would respond to the lack of affordable childcare for low- or moderate-income people, including a high percentage of single parents.

Thus, four new programs—a community clinic, senior center, child care center, and food bank—took root in the farmers' market to serve downtown residents. Under Zaretsky and Hurley's guidance, citizen groups developed each of the four agencies' goals and planned their physical facilities. The PDA was awarded $550,000 to build and establish two projects—a

community health clinic and a senior center—and then stood back and let citizen efforts bloom. The PDA would provide institutional support, including Zaretsky's salary, legal and accounting services, and Market space at reduced rents. Each of the four new agencies organized as an independent non-profit corporation reflecting the commitment to self-help and self-determination.

Zaretsky got a stark sense of how much community excitement had been generated. He couldn't find anyone

Neglected and alone, many low-income downtown residents living near the Market were without social services when Zaretsky and Hurley came on board for the PDA. Most wanted health care and a place to get together, a "living room in the Market." (Facing page, top: The Market Foundation, photo by Lynn Hamrick; Facing page, middle: Seattle Times file, 1988, photo by Betty Udesen; Facing page, bottom: The Market Foundation, photo by John Stamets; Above: The Market Foundation, photo by Victor Gardaya)

who wanted to wait the two years for the health clinic and senior center construction to be completed. Temporary quarters were sought and gin rummy playing grandmas replaced Hell's Angels bikers as the principal occupants in what had once been the Motherlode Tavern. Zaretsky admits, "It was a rat hole. With only $500 to start, dozens of people worked to make it usable—scrubbing 40 years worth of spilled beer and cigarette smoke off the walls and floors, repairing, painting, and rebuilding. . . . The bar was transformed into the social gathering place for the Senior Center and the men's restroom became the Clinic's lab. The rest was divided into exam rooms and space for other services. From day one, the Motherlode was filled with community people who came because it was 'their' space."

PIKE MARKET COMMUNITY CLINIC

The Pike Market Community Clinic began providing limited nursing services in June of 1978—several weeks before it opened in the Motherlode. With the spilled beer scrubbed away and the temporary facility a reality, the Clinic offered physician services on a regular part-time basis. Two federal programs, Volunteers in Service to America (VISTA) and Comprehensive Education and Training Act (CETA), provided the Clinic's first staff positions. Despite the unusual surroundings, the patient load grew steadily.

The construction of the new facility was completed in October 1979, and by that time, the Clinic's patient population had grown sufficiently to require full-time operation. From the beginning, it emphasized treatment to those over 65, many suffering from one or more chronic conditions such as diabetes and heart disease. Today, cost of the care is subsidized by the Clinic, since many live on limited pensions and social security.

PIKE MARKET SENIOR CENTER

The initial Motherlode location was only one sign that the organizers of the Pike Market Senior Center clearly did not want a typical senior center. The founding group of volunteers wanted to establish the Center more as an extended family than a social service. They hoped the Center would make it easy for people to get out of their small rooms into a comfortable "living room" setting that encouraged interaction. This concern set many

FACING PAGE, ABOVE: *Clinic staff, in 1980, pose at the entrance in solidarity to improve the lives of Market residents. (The Market Foundation)*

FACING PAGE, BELOW: *Joe Martin, a clinic social worker, and Florence, a clinic patient, at the Pike Market Community Clinic. (The Market Foundation, photo by Gary Sutto)*

ABOVE: *The Pike Place Market Senior Center, like most organizations in the Market, is run by a board of users rather than social services professionals. (The Market Foundation)*

of the Center's priorities—like the decision not to allow television. It also drove the desire for a community kitchen where seniors could throw parties, celebrate holidays, and put together potlucks. The Center would provide classes and other activities that build a sense of community involvement and offer a place for people watching with views of the street.

The strong feeling of community ownership continues. The Senior Center is still run by a board of users rather than social service professionals and many of its programs are possible only through the contributions of its many user-volunteers.

PIKE MARKET CHILD CARE AND PRESCHOOL

The frustrations of finding good, affordable child care in downtown Seattle led to the establishment of the Pike Market Child Care and Preschool in 1982. From its inception, the Center has been committed to serving low-income families living downtown and Market merchants, farmers, and craftspeople. Although it

started later than the Clinic and Senior Center, the Child Care and Preschool evolved in much the same way. The PDA provided staff support and fundraising, but took direction from parents and volunteers in the definition and organization of the Center.

And like the other projects, adversity spawned community spirit and action. Federal funds had been secured for the construction of an outdoor play area, without which the Center would not be permitted to open. When Uncle Sam walked away from the commitment, concerned citizens organized a private campaign to raise the necessary funds.

Each year, children aged eighteen months through five years from one hundred families attend Pike Market Child Care and Preschool, which charges on a sliding scale based on family size and income. The Child Care and Preschool program includes a mix of educational and structured play activities—arts and crafts, swimming lessons, music and singing, and exercises to develop reading and writing skills. The Market itself is a key educational resource and the staff works to capitalize on the Center's location by seeing the Market as a "microcosm of the city."

DOWNTOWN FOOD BANK

The Downtown Food Bank was started in 1979, in a public housing project (the Morrison Hotel), by Richard Brooks. Brooks initially collected food donations from Market vendors in his shopping cart. It quickly became apparent that more people needed the services of the Food Bank than had been anticipated, making it imperative to find another home. The Senior Center was a logical partner as many Center users also used the Food Bank. The Downtown Food Bank has operated under the legal and fiscal auspices of the Senior Center since 1980. Since 1989, the Food Bank has been located on the 5th level of the Public Market parking garage.

Says a volunteer, "I've been working at the Food Bank for five years now and I've seen all kinds of people come through—old folks, single parents, people who just lost their job. What do I think of the Food Bank? We sure do need it down here." Food Bank recipients are typically eligible for only minimum public benefits, and many have experienced cutbacks in what little they do receive. Many younger people use the Food Bank as a last resort, coming only after exhausting all available unemployment benefits. Food Bank staff members have found that having an elderly constituency is an advantage in fundraising and outreach efforts.

THE MARKET FOUNDATION GROWS

The impressive uphill climb of the four Market agencies—Senior Center, Clinic, Food Bank, and Child Care and Preschool—made during the 1970s was

threatened by the downhill trend of federal support in the 1980s. Senator Warren G. Magnuson, a longtime Market supporter, lost his seat and newly elected President Ronald Reagan announced budget cuts that reduced agency support as well as the money for building rehabilitation. 50 percent of the total funding available or promised to the agencies

FACING PAGE: *The Pike Market Child Care and Preschool serves low-income families living downtown, market merchants, farmers, and craftspeople. Kids soon learned to love the excitement of the Market. (The Market Foundation, photo by John Stamets)*

ABOVE: *"I've been working at the Food Bank for five years now and I've seen all kinds of people come through—old folks, single parents, people who just lost their job. . . . What do I think of the Food Bank? We sure do need it down here," said a Downtown Food Bank volunteer. (The Market Foundation; photo by John Stamets)*

a private fundraising drive to establish a "mini-park" play area, which is still a Market fixture decades later. It became clear that the reasons people donated to the campaign had little to do with child care. They gave because—like all Seattleites—they loved the Market. When Illsley Nordstrom, a member of a major Seattle retailing family, agreed to contribute to the play park project, she talked of her personal joy in the Market and her understanding of it as a key institution in the fabric of downtown. When she asked what she could do to help maintain its vitality, it became clear that the Market had no way to regularly gain the support of those who well understood how much it means to the City.

Nordstrom's questions helped Hurley and Zaretsky understand that people's strong affection for the Market could provide the underpinning of ongoing support for all four Market agencies. The citywide love for the Market could and would be reflected in a foundation, which would ensure the long-term survival of the Market's human services.

The idea of a cooperative fundraising effort to raise money for the Market's agencies had been considered earlier, but this time the need to get the programs off the funding roller coaster carried the day. With the exception of hospitals, significant private fundraising on behalf of neighborhood social service agencies was almost unheard of at the time. The idea was not to have bake sales and car washes, but to cover the agencies' combined $400,000 operating deficit. Zaretsky and Hurley met with twenty-five enthusiastic downtown business people. Plans to create the new Market Foundation began.

Fresh from helping to open the new mini-park to delighted four-year-olds, Jean Falls was asked to establish a Steering Committee. This committee,

vanished.

At the same time, tough economic times increased demand for services. Elliott Bronstein, program director of the Senior Center said: "As soon as the budget cuts hit we experienced a 20 percent escalation in the number of people who walked through the door every day. The following month, the number grew another 10 percent. There was a greater demand on all services but especially the survival services—food, daytime shelter, and referrals for food stamps, social security, and housing. We were strapped."

It was at the Child Care and Preschool where necessity first drove the highest level of invention. Longtime Market supporters, Jean Falls and Mary Fleming, gave birth to the idea of the Market Foundation as they organized

comprised of members of Seattle's corporate and philanthropic communities, wrote the statement of purpose, drafted Articles of Incorporation, filed for tax-exempt status with the IRS, and developed a list of candidates for the Foundation's first Board of Directors.

The PDA played the same strong support role that Zaretsky had exhibited two years previously, providing office space, staff, equipment, and the moral support crucial to the Market Foundation's development. Two VISTA volunteers were hired by the PDA to assist in the start-up phase and to recruit Market Foundation board members. Marlys Erickson and Peggy Boyer started work in January 1982. Erickson said, "We used the "arts" model of finding board members: someone knows a banker, another person knows a lawyer, and another knows a business owner." By that summer, a group of board members with personal connections and a deep commitment to the Market was assembled.

Each Market Foundation board member was also chosen to represent either the corporate, philanthropic, or arts leadership in Seattle. Business community leaders included Pike Place Market merchants; representatives from major regional companies; and professionals in public relations, law, and architecture. Within the Market social service community there were fierce debates about the composition of this board. Some felt it should be more community based, more directly reflecting the constituency served. The argument that prevailed assumed the Market Foundation's strength would lie in its ability to raise

---

ABOVE: *At the annual Market Foundation "cut of the pie" celebration, checks are handed out to the Market's social service agencies. Here, Gerry Johnson (Market Foundation President from 1985 to 1988) is at the podium. Behind him in trench coat is David Wright, the first Foundation Board President. (The Market Foundation)*

FACING PAGE, ABOVE: *Leaders of the Market Foundation's first capital campaign, Bill Randall and Judy Runstad, pose with Rachel, the Foundation's icon. (The Market Foundation)*

FACING PAGE, BELOW: *Few visitors to the Market realize that the "real" Rachel, a 750-lb. bruiser of a pig, won the 1985 Island County Fair prize and lived contentedly on Whidbey Island to a ripe old age. After gaining the attention of Whidbey Islanders, the "real" Rachel modeled for sculptor Georgia Gerber as she sculpted a cast for a life-size bronze replica. The "real" Rachel traveled once to the Pike Place Market to visit her bronze namesake. (The Market Foundation)*

money and that its effectiveness would depend on close ties to regional corporate and philanthropic communities.

The Board of Directors held its first meeting on August 17, 1982, the seventy-fifth anniversary of the Pike Place Market. It was a replay of the Market's opening day as members of Seattle's citizen and business leadership gathered in Jean Falls's Highlands home.

In each of its first two full years, the Foundation distributed $40,000 to the Market agencies, attracting significant local support from Seattle's downtown Kiwanis. In 1985, its third year, the Foundation leapt forward, generating $158,000, including $50,000 from the first membership drive. By 2005, in its twenty-fourth year, the Market Foundation disbursed nearly $2 million to Market programs and capital projects, including $970,000 to build a new Senior Center,

with memories of Hell's Angels and beer-stained bars now faded. And year after year the Market Foundation and its friends have outdone themselves with creative ideas for supporting the Senior Center, Food Bank, Clinic, and Child Care and Preschool.

With the PDA, the Foundation helped to mount a campaign to raise $1.2 million to resurface the Market's floor. Eight to ten million people tread on the Market's floor each year, wearing out the surface. Repair and replacement was accomplished by selling individual tiles. Donors paid $35 to have the name of their choice imprinted on a quarry tile. In July 1985, 45,000 tiles went on sale; by the end of January 1986, they were sold out. The $1.2 million raised paid for the actual costs of repaving the floor and raised $100,000 to begin the Market Foundation endowment.

In August 1986, the Foundation installed a bronze, life-sized piggybank modeled after a 750-pound sow named Rachel, a prizewinner at the Island County Fair. Rachel was sculpted by Pacific Northwest artist Georgia Gerber. Located under the Market clock at Pike Place and Pike, Rachel raises $9,000 a year in quarters, lira, shillings, and coins from Market visitors from around the world.

In 1989, the PDA and the Market Foundation worked jointly to develop Heritage House, an assisted living residence for 96 frail seniors. Heritage House, operated by the Sisters of Providence, resides on top of the Market's parking garage.

In the summer of 2001, as homage to Rachel, 170 decorated fiberglass life-size pigs were installed on the City of Seattle streets. The "Pigs on Parade" campaign raised Pike Place Market awareness and the auction of the pigs was one of Seattle's livelier bidding wars, that brought $500,000 to the Market Foundation's endowment. In 2005 the Market Foundation took over sponsorship of the Pike Place Street Fair. On Memorial Day weekend, more than 80,000 people roamed the Pike Place Market, many contributing money through giant pink pigs placed throughout the Fair.

While sustaining a diverse community in the Pike Place Market is the responsibility of many, the Market Foundation is an important force in assuring a continued commitment to the goals of the 1971 "Keep the Market" initiative. Constant vigilance is required to maintain the vision of a vital Market that embraces a low-income community. The Foundation has assumed an advocacy role, fighting to protect the human character of the Market and thus the City's soul. The energy of the Market Foundation works to counteract the inevitable inertia that many feared would prevail after the completion of the Market's physical renovation. As Jean Falls reminds us, "The Market needs people to worry about it. It shouldn't ever seem to be going too well or it will get away from us."

Worry yes, but Jean and her colleagues could celebrate as well. In 1985, the Pike Place Market won the first national competition for Excellence in the Urban Environment, the Rudy Bruner award. The award committee said,

> Pike Place emerged as a winner partly because it has become a place for nearly everyone—for the low-income elderly who have long lived in the downtown area, for the area's farmers, for independent business operators, for artists and craftspeople, for local entertainers, for downtown workers, for gourmets, for middle-class people, for some wealthy people, and for tourists.

In 2007, the Foundation celebrated its twenty-fifth anniversary. By then, it had given more than $12 million to the Market's human services and heritage programs, run two successful capital campaigns, coordinated the twenty-fifth anniversary of the Market initiative, built the Market Heritage Center, and initiated programs to assist Market farmers. The Foundation spearheaded efforts to build an addition to the LaSalle Hotel, home to a new Senior Center, and doubled the number of exam rooms at the Pike Market Clinic. At the beginning of 2007, the Foundation raised the corporate

ABOVE: *Bronze hooves lead the way to Rachel, at the Pike Street sidewalk entrance to the Market. The hooves were installed during the second Market Foundation capital campaign in 1996. (The Market Foundation)*

FACING PAGE: *"Become a legend in your own tile," was the campaign slogan for the popular tile campaign to pave the floor of the Pike Place Market arcade. (The Market Foundation)*

Epilogue

When veterans of the initiative campaign and the litigation gathered at the Market to commemorate victory, few found the Market of their early memory, none the Market of their vision. Each regretted some change, some hope lost in compromise, but for all there was the satisfaction of a battle won, a

Republic. Councilman Thomas Revelle thought that by providing Seattle's yeoman producers with a place to sell their crops directly to consumers, industry would provide manufacturing goods to the tillers of the soil and the Market "would cause apparently sterile fields to blossom as the rose." Frank Goodwin sought to create an area of pragmatic simplicity, where producer and consumer might meet in surroundings "not too costly in appearance or so decorative in ornamentation that it would have a tendency to discourage trade among patrons who are drawn to the Market because of the necessity of saving on the purchase of foods." Willard Soames fought for the farmers' right to have some say in Market governance. Doc Brown preached municipal ownership. Joe Desimone practiced the practical paternalism of a democratic boss. Mark Tobey celebrated the humanity of the Market regulars. Victor and Peter Steinbrueck saw the peril and clarioned the alarm. Thousands responded.

In the Market of today, altered but recognizable, a place of glowing produce and friendly vendors, with vistas sometimes of gray water and misty mountains, sometimes of sun dazzle, sometimes of a floodlit ferry gliding in a sea of darkness, of aisles lined with restaurants offering exotic foods and good doughnuts, local wines and imported beers, alive with shoppers of every pigment and garb, a motley of panhandlers, baby-packing teenagers, cops, street musicians, antiquarians, peddlers of pots and kitsch, herbs, whatnot and whimsy, an endless line of people seeking bargains, people seeking the unique or finest quality, people whose only aim is to join the flow, or observe it—in the continuum lies the victory still celebrated by all friends of the Market.

disaster averted. While there was a great deal more work to do, they had helped preserve not merely a cluster of buildings on a cliff above an inland sea, but the embodiment of a people's aspiration.

Thomas Jefferson imagined the independent yeoman raising crops on his own soil to be the hope and purpose of the

Related Reading

Birkeland, Torger. *Echoes of Puget Sound: Fifty Years of Logging and Steamboating.* Caldwell, Idaho: Caxton Printers, 1961.

Evans, Jack R. *Little History of Pike Place Market.* Seattle: SCW Publications, 1991.

Focke, Anne. *Sustaining a Vital Downtown Community: A Study of the Market Foundation.* Seattle: The Market Foundation, 1987.

Gee, Nancie. *Reflections in Pike Place Market.* Seattle: Superior Publishing, 1968.

Goodwin, Arthur. *Markets: Public and Private.* Seattle: Montgomery Printing, 1929.

Kitagawa, Daisuke. *Issei and Nissei: The Internment Years.* New York: Seabury Press, 1967.

Morgan, Murray. *Skid Road: An Informal Portrait of Seattle.* 2nd rev. ed. Seattle: University of Washington Press, 1982.

Olin, Laurie. *Breath on the Mirror: Seattle's Skid Road Community.* Seattle, 1972.

Pelligrini, Angelo. *Immigrant's Return.* New York: Macmillan, 1951.

Pike Place Market Foundation. *Pigs on Parade.* Seattle: Marathon Group, 2001.

Pike Place Market Merchants' Association. *The Market Notebook.* Seattle: Pike Place Market Merchants' Association, 1978.

Pike Place Market Preservation and Development Authority. *Pike Place Market: 100 Years.* Seattle: Sasquatch Books, 2007

Potts, Ralph B., and Lowell S. Hawley. *Counsel for the Damned.* Philadelphia: J. B. Lippincott, 1953.

Rex-Johnson, Braiden. *Pike Place Market Cookbook.* Seattle: Sasquatch Books, 2003.

Rex-Johnson, Braiden. *Pike Place Market Seafood Cookbook.* Berkeley: Ten Speed Press, 2005.

Rex-Johnson, Braiden, and Paul Souders. *Inside the Pike Place Market: Exploring America's Favorite Farmer's Market.* Seattle: Sasquatch Books, 1999.

Sale, Roger. *Seattle: Past to Present.* Seattle: University of Washington Press, 1976.

Sharp, Joan, Walter Hatch, and Will Hatch. *Good Pride: A Story of the Pike Place Market Farmers.* Seattle: Market Oral History Project, 1982.

Spitzer, Theodore Morrow, and Hilary Baum. *Public Markets and Community Revitalization.* Washington, D.C.: Urban Land Institute and Project for Public Spaces, 1995.

Stamets, John. *Portrait of a Market: Photographs of Seattle's Pike Place Market.* Seattle: Real Comet Press, 1987.

Steinbrueck, Victor. *Market Sketchbook: 25th Anniversary Edition.* Seattle: University of Washington Press, 1996.

Tobey, Mark. *The World of a Market.* Seattle: University of Washington Press, 1964.

Wehrwein, George S. *Public Markets in the State of Washington.* Pullman, Washington: Washington State College, 1918.

Yaeger, Michael, and Sarah Clementson. *An Insider's Tour of the Market.* Seattle: Studio Solstone, 1991.

Yokoyama, John, and Joseph Michelli. *When Fish Fly: Lessons for Creating a Vital and Energized Workplace–From the World Famous Pike Place Fish Market.* New York: Hyperion, 2004.